HEALING MUSIC

HEALING MUSIC

Andrew Watson & Nevill Drury

Special thanks are due to Judith Hemsley and Claire Leimbach for their assistance in preparing the visualisation sections of this manuscript. Thanks also to Dr Manfred Clynes for reviewing the material on sentics.

First published in Australasia in 1987 by
Nature & Health Books
This edition co-published in Great Britain by
Prism Press, 2 South Street, Bridport,
Dorset DT6 3NQ, England
and distributed in the United States of America by
the Avery Publishing Group Inc.,
350 Thorens Avenue, Garden City Park, New York, 11040

ISBN 1 85327 002 4

Design: Craig Peterson
Typeset by Setila Type Studio, Sydney
Printed in Australia by The Book Printer

CONTENTS

INTRODUCTION

This book was born of necessity. There is simply so much interest in the healing powers of music, and in New Age music specifically, that we felt compelled to write this book for those readers drawn to this area of human experience.

In a sense, the book is both practical and descriptive. The sort of blend we have sought is an overview of holistic health and visualisation coupled with practical self-help exercises and lists of New Age music. After all, preventive health is essentially about self-help – people want increasingly to become involved in the processes of becoming well and staying well – and this book is aimed at people with this priority.

Music, of course, provides the focus and here, as writers, we took two different roles. Andrew Watson works as a healer and natural therapist and he contributed chapters three, four and five – which describe energy levels in the human organism and visualisations based on the chakras. Nevill Drury has for many years been a reviewer of New Age music and is a writer/editor in the area of mind and body therapies. He contributed the first two chapters, which deal with the concept of 'healing music' and basic principles of holistic health, and he also wrote chapter six – an international overview of New Age music. Much of this chapter appeared in Nevill's earlier book *Music for Inner Space*, but since that book was published in 1985 many more New Age musicians have appeared on the scene, and it was necessary to update the information in various places.

We also hope readers will find the Appendices useful. These feature descriptive information on albums suitable as aids to healing and creative visualisation, and also reviews of some of the leading musicians in the genre. Also included in this part of the book are listings of specific pieces of music that correlate with the Elements so if you are looking for music to enhance a 'water' meditation or an 'earth', 'fire' or 'spirit' visualisation in yoga (among many other possibilities) this section will hopefully provide some useful leads for you to pursue.

Finally, we hope that this book will help you tune into the basic concept of healing through music. As Auerbach said, 'Music washes away from the soul the dust of everyday life.'

What an inspiring idea for re-visioning the 1980s!

1 WHAT IS HEALING MUSIC?

For those of us who live in cities, the world is an extremely noisy place. Imagine this typical suburban scenario:

7.30 am.	Awaken to the sound of squabbling children, barking dogs, early commuter traffic, inane radio talk-shows over breakfast.
8.30 am.	Travel to work: screeching brakes, the din of train or highway, verbal irritations from fellow travellers, the yell of newspaper vendors proclaiming the latest sensational headline, foggy and incoherent announcements blasting forth from platform loud-speakers or forceful, overstated advertisements on the car radio.
9.00-5.00 pm.	Constant background noise from the office air-conditioner, the periodic shrill of tone signals from a cluster of phones, and the seemingly constant click-clack of secretarial typewriters...

And so it all goes on, fractured perhaps by the throaty roar of lawnmowers on the weekend...

Clearly it would not be difficult to imagine oneself swamped in an ocean of urban noise as a logical consequence of our modern western lifestyle. Noise is all around us, impinging on our privacy, shattering the calm, leaving our nerves on edge. Little wonder that increasingly more and more people are turning to techniques of stress control, relaxation and meditation. Little wonder, indeed, that more and more people feel the need to tap an inner resource of peace and stillness.

The urge towards inner peace – or inner health, for it amounts to that – has manifested in many different ways. It is mirrored in the continuing western popularity of yoga and mysticism and the gradual emergence of the holistic model of health – a model which emphasises the interrelatedness of body, mind and spirit. It is reflected in the belief that a degenerative disease like cancer, which is the result of a breakdown in the body's immune system, may be treated with meditation instead of chemotherapy. It also manifests in the ever-burgeoning league of spiritual gurus – authority figures of varying hues and colours, most of whom in their own distinctive ways point the way to the calm in the centre of the cyclone. And it is mirrored too by the rise of what we are calling *healing music* – music specifically conceived as an adjunct to visualisation or meditation exercises and designed to enhance one's feeling of inner well-being.

It has to be said that there are many different notions of just what types of music can be used for healing or therapeutic purpose. Some therapists link music specifically to mood, others consider the direct impact of sound on the cells of the body, and still others have developed ways of linking music to visual imagery in order to stimulate a variety of responses from the subconscious mind. The approaches range from intuitive and metaphysical interpretations of music through to purely scientific neurological models. Other systems, like applied kinesiology – which blends western psychology with eastern concepts of energy flow – hover somewhere in between.

Sound and Music

Perhaps it is best to begin by asking how the impact of sound affects the senses. The range of human hearing extends from 16-20,000 cycles per second and this is known as the 'sonic range'. Below that level are inaudible, sub-sonic frequencies and beyond it, the range of vibrations referred to as the ultra-sonic spectrum. The impact of sound perceived by the human ear is measured in decibels – recorded as dbA – and it is generally estimated by the Occupational Safety and Health Administration in the United States that the maximum sound intensity that one can be exposed to over an 8-hour period without incurring hearing loss is 75 dbA. General street noise often averages 80 dbA, and the volume at rock concerts, especially of the 'heavy metal' kind, may exceed 90 dbA. Even orchestral performances of music by Wagner or Beethoven – who rank among the more dramatic and powerful composers – may exceed 85 dbA. So volume thresholds are definitely one area to consider.

Another factor in sound is rhythm. Some rhythmic patterns in music have the ability to sweep us along with their momentum, to elevate us to a new level of sensory awareness. Such forms of music, as Carl Seashore notes in his *Psychology of Music,* produce 'a mild form of ecstasy' or 'a feeling of freedom, luxury and expanse.' *Other rhythmic patterns, especially the anapestic stopped beat of some forms of rock music – da : da : DA – may have a draining or weakening effect on the human organism. This is certainly the view of psychiatrist Dr John Diamond, who believes that this particular beat results in loss of symmetry between the two cerebral hemispheres of the brain, resulting in 'subtle perceptual difficulties and a host of other early manifestations of stress.' In such an instance, he continues, 'the entire body is thrown into a state of alarm.'**

Still another factor in considering sound is the difference between the rate of body vibration and the impact of in-coming frequencies. As American pianist and musicologist Dr Steven Halpern writes in *Sound Health*, the body cells rarely vibrate at more than 1000 cycles per second, whereas the range of sound perception extends to 20,000 cycles per second. The body therefore has to filter a broad range of incoming sounds and acts like a type of vibratory transformer. Sometimes this can be extremely stressful.

For example, specific sound frequencies like TV 'hum', which resonates at 15,750 cycles per second and permeates the room quite stealthily, can have a pro-

**Carl Seashore: 1967 p 142 **John Diamond: 1979 p 103*

nounced draining effect on the body – quite apart from the more noticeable and tangible impact of bombastic commercials.

Sound, of course, is quite different to music – although at times the distinction can get blurred at the edges. Cultural factors may be involved too: for example, to some western ears the intense beat of primitive African congas or the unfamiliar scales of Middle Eastern music may seem alien and unappealing – a range of intrusive sounds rather than 'sweet music to the ears'. One also hears similar comments made by parents about pop music! However, these things are purely personal, and tastes will vary.

Nevertheless, without judging music to be either 'good' or 'bad' one can say perhaps, that music may be distinguished from sound by containing meaning and purpose for the listener. One could also add that it has the capacity, through the associations it evokes, to transform consciousness.

Music may also be distinguished from sound by the range of its distinctive qualities which account for the rich aesthetic quality of musical experience.

Here are some of the qualities in music which affect us as listeners:

Pitch – This refers to the frequency of the music, the number of vibrations in a given sound. Rapid vibrations produce a strong nervous stimulus, slower vibrations tend to relax.

Intensity – This relates to the amplitude of vibrations. Loud music has considerable 'carrying power' – it is dominating and coercive, excludes other sounds and may give the listener the feeling of being 'protected'. Soft music, on the other hand, is more intimate and serene.

Timbre – Also known as 'tone colour'. This depends on the harmonies in the music and evokes associations in the mind of the listener at a non-intellectual level.

Interval – This refers to the distance between notes and results in melody and harmony. Certain combinations of notes will seem more attractive but, as we mentioned earlier, this type of evaluation is largely influenced by cultural factors.

Rhythm – This is the dynamic element in music – the time pattern within a certain speed. 'Standard' rhythm is roughly the same rate as the heart-beat: around 70 or 80 beats a minute. Rhythm relates strongly to different human emotions.

Perceptual quality – Music is a non-verbal form of expression and is perceived through the auditory apparatus in the ear and then channelled to areas of emotional responses in the brain, some of which are associated with the limbic system. Music helps to stimulate – imagination, fantasy, and intuition and thus helps to integrate the functions of left and right hemispheres.

So there are many aspects to consider in music, and a wide variety of possible individual responses. The intriguing thing is that exactly how music communicates emotions can be scientifically measured, as research scientist Dr Manfred Clynes has discovered.

The Sentic Cycles of Dr Manfred Clynes

Dr Manfred Clynes was born in Vienna and as a musician studied with Pablo Casals and Sascha Gorodniszki. He holds a doctorate in neuroscience and engineering from the University of Melbourne and a master's degree from the Juilliard School in New York. He is also head of the Research Centre at the New South Wales Conservatorium of Music, so his credentials are impressive.

Basically, Dr Clynes has shown that emotions exist in their own right as potential patterns in the nervous system and can be triggered by music in a general way, quite independently of specific associations with people or events. This means, in effect, that certain passages of music, according to the shape of the musical phrases in their structure, can generate such responses as joy, sadness, love or reverence.

The composer is able to tap what Clynes has termed 'essentic forms' – basic emotional 'shapes' which relate to feelings – and it is these shapes which fill the notes in the composition. The musical tones are pitched at different points along the path of the essentic form, acting as markers towards the generation of that form.

According to Clynes also, several of the great classical composers like Mozart, Beethoven, Schubert or Brahms, produced a characteristic pulse which became the hallmark of their work – a reflection of their unique identity and creativity. And it is the musical pulse which does much to determine the subtle character of the music.

What this means is that music is much greater than the sum of its most obvious constituents – it also involves what Clynes calls 'microstructure'. Structure and microstructure, says Clynes are 'an indissoluble unity... a reflection of the subtlety of our own nature. As we study its subtlety we are amazed at the seemingly unlimited ability to evoke meaningful musical qualities in their pure form.

'This wealth to be unearthed is in fact the secret of art, and is also its power to suffuse our state with transcendent experience... (the experience) includes empathy with the being of the composer and the extension with all beings – proof that the most intimately personal is also the most universal.'*

According to Clynes, the musical expression of joy, sadness or love requires not only a certain spacing in time and pitch but also that the amplitudes in the music follow an appropriate essentic form. The more effectively the form is realised in a musical composition, the greater its impact on the listener. As Clynes says, 'It can touch the heart as directly as a physical touch.'›

Dr Clynes has also found that there is an important therapeutic application which arises from his discovery of essentic forms. Basically, if the essentic forms are repeatedly expressed, it makes it easier for a person to feel or re-learn those emotions. After several years of testing and refinement, Clynes arrived at what he now calls the Standard Cycle of Emotions.

This cycle consists of seven emotions : anger, hate, grief, love, sex, joy and reverence, and each of these emotions has a characteristic span of expression ranging from 4.8 seconds (anger) to 9.8 seconds (reverence). In a therapeutic setting, individuals use simple finger pressure expressions for each of the emotions while they sit in a straight-backed chair listening to a tape which provides the timing. Through exploring the emotions in turn, each individual learns to explore the range of personal emotions and releases pent-up tension. The essentic forms thus provide an important tool for overcoming emotional blocks.

Each of the essentic forms can be graphically depicted on the basis of finger pressure and each has a characteristic shape:

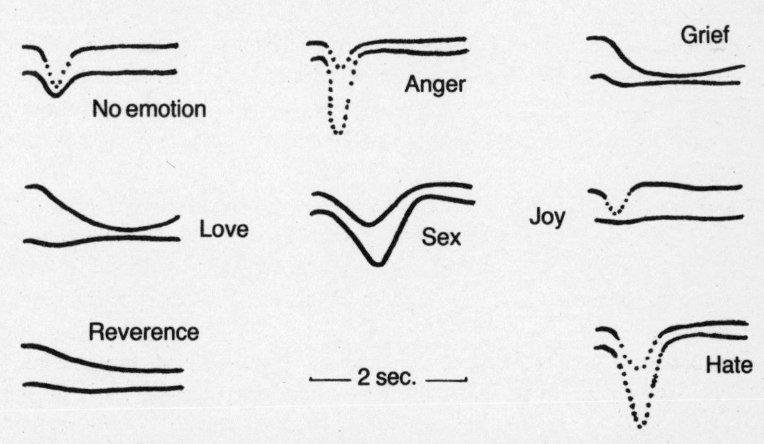

When Clynes asks people to push a button while they experience particular feelings, the patterns of pressure on the button approximate these averaged 'pure' forms (essentic forms). The upper lines represent downward-upward pressure, the lower lines forward-backward pressure.

**Brain/Mind Bulletin January 21, 1985 p. 3* ›*Ibid, p. 5*

After working with the sentic cycles for even a short time, people learn how easy it is to access and express basic emotions. Also, each session typically ends with a feeling of calmness and peace. As Clynes' colleague Stoyan Jurisevic notes in a recent article on Clynes' work, 'There is a deep wisdom in the emotions which, to the degree to which we have cut ourselves off from our feelings, we are blind to, and it is a wisdom which we need to rediscover if we are to be human in our personal relationships and social structures.'*

The Power of Rhythm

Several music researchers have highlighted the significance not only of structure but also of rhythm. It is obvious, if we pause to reflect, that in the physical universe rhythm is central to our existence. Rhythm is a feature of the basic pulsing structure of electrons and a characteristic of our breathing-running-walking patterns, the beat of our hearts, and the very structure of our speech patterns. And there are many reasons why this should be so, for as musicologist Craigie Macfie writes in his article 'Music and Medicine': 'Perhaps our response to rhythm is biologically determined, both in terms of our very early exposure to the rhythms of the maternal heart-beat and respiration, and as a result of our nervous system's need to simplify our sensory environment into comprehensible units.'

Rhythm also has other important characteristics. As Carl Seashore notes, it may give rise to a feeling of balance or symmetry, or on other occasions provide a surge of power: 'It is like a dream of flying; it is so easy to soar...' Indeed, it can often seem as if the rhythm in the music resonates with one's whole being.

Again quoting Seashore:

'Rhythm, whether in perception or action, is emotional when highly developed, and results in the response of the whole organism to its pulsations. Such organic pulsations and secretions are the physical counterpart of emotion. Thus when we listen to the dashing billows or the trickling raindrops, when we see the swaying of the trees in the wind or the waving of the wheat fields, we respond to these, we feel ourselves into them, and there is rhythm everywhere, not only in every plastic part of our body, but in the world as we know it at the moment.'**

So music and rhythm reflect the very pulse of life, and to the extent that we ourselves respond to the rhythms of music, we engage in the rhythms of the natural universe. We resonate with them, and the energies of life and creativity flow through us.

Music and Image

Terence McLaughlin, author of *Music and Communication*, has highlighted what

**Stoyan Jurisevic : 1984 p. 87 ** Carl Seashore: 1967 p. 144*

many of us know intuitively – that 'music may suggest colours, colours may suggest taste or touch.' And our language has numerous phrases which reflect this tendency, as when we speak of 'dry, white wine', 'cold blue sky' or the 'warm tones of someone's voice'. McLaughlin suggests in fact that such aspects of the human condition as hunger-satiety, pain-pleasure, grief-solace, desire-orgasm can be seen in terms of tension and resolution and that music has the capacity to express this resolution in a way which verbal communication cannot. Craigie McFie agrees: 'It has an infinite capacity to act as a subtle metaphor,' he writes, and is able 'to suggest associations and to progress simultaneously along lines of both logical thinking and the "primary process" thinking of dreams.'

We are encroaching now on another dimension of music, and one which is frequently used by healers and therapists – the ability of music to evoke or enhance visual imagery. For so often it is the image in the mind's eye which becomes a vehicle for self-transformation, allowing the subject to imagine himself passing from a state of conflict and tension to holistic well-being. This idea is in fact the basic thrust of this book, for our primary focus is on music which can assist the healing process.

It is not surprising that music and imagery are linked, for the musician himself dwells in a world of images. As one writer has put it, the composer creates music 'by hearing it out in his creative imagination through his "mind's ear". That is, his memory and imagination are rich and strong in power of concrete, faithful and vivid tonal imagery; this imagery is so fully at his command that he can build the most complex musical structures and hear and feel all the effects of every detailed element before he has written down a note or sounded it out by voice or instrument. This capacity… is the outstanding mark of a musical mind at the representational level – the capacity of living in a representational tonal world. Take out the image from the musical mind and you take out its very essence.' *

The special gift of the musician is in fact the ability to transmit mental images to the listener through his music. As Stephen McAdams writes in his article 'Spectral Fusion and the Creation of Auditory Images', 'The composer creates a universe within which the listener can create musical worlds and forms. The composer enfolds a universe, the listener unfolds a new music and is unfolded by a new music with each coming-into-being of the sounds of that universe.'**

Alfred Nieman, writing in the *British Journal of Music Therapy* says much the same thing:

'Images (in music) are crystallised by the composer into shapes like a melody or a rhythmic figure having some kind of harmonic or textural implication. This is how they are received by the listener – a melody or figure in time. The unconscious

**Carl Seashore: 1967, p6 **Stephen McAdams: 1982, p296*

mind receiving them acts as a catalyst and returns the music back to its original symbolic nature.'*

Music is also a wonderful stimulus to the imagination, as Juliette Alvin notes in her classic book on music therapy:

'Imagination is one of the most creative faculties of man when it is kept within reasonable bounds. Since music is wordless there are few limits to its evocative and imaginative power. Day-dreaming, imagery, mental flights into an invisible world have been part of the musical experiences of man and are non-intellectual.'**

Elaborating this point she goes on to say:

'The power of music to evoke images or sensations can explain its association with psychic states in which individuality, time and space disappear or take another dimension.'***

This in itself is an intriguing and mysterious process in which the ego is put to one side and one simply *receives*, or acts as a channel. Christopher Gaynor expresses it very well when he writes:

'Awaking into song a discovery of a voice that we don't own, *a voice coming through us.* I give up "my" voice *in order that the world may sing through me.* To stand naked in the music is to let it enter our pores, to wash over pre-conceptions of what we think the music is.'**** (our italics)

Music thus opens us to new universes, to new dimensions of being that many of us have ignored in our daily lives. It is precisely this remarkable quality of music that lends itself to the healing process, for in the type of healing we are thinking of here, music helps draw into the mind and body the inner resources of the spirit. It is almost like drawing on the music of the spheres for our medicine...

The Healing Power of Music

The ancient Greeks were among the first to develop the idea that music could be used to heal. Aristotle believed that flute music could arouse strong emotions and thus often lead to a state of cathartic release. Zithers were played by the ancient Greeks as an accompaniment to meals to aid digestion, and according to Cassiodorus, the Aeolian mode of music could be used to treat mental disturbance and induce sleep. The Lydian mode, often considered ideal for children, was intended to 'soothe the soul when oppressed with excessive care.'*****

But it was Pythagoras who developed the concept of healing through melodic intervals and rhythms. We have no way of knowing exactly what the music sounded like, but we do have an account of his work at Crotona. It comes from the

---

* *Alfred Nieman: 1973, pp2-7* ** *Juliette Alvin: 1975, p83*

*** *Ibid, p. 84* **** *Christopher Gaynor in Stephen McAdams: 1982 p. 296*

***** *Juliette Alvin: 1975 p. 84*

writings of Iamblichus, the noted neoplatonist and mystic, and it is so interesting that we quote it here at length:

'Conceiving that the first attention which should be paid to men is that which takes place through the senses, as when someone perceives beautiful figures and forms or hears beautiful rhythms and melodies, Pythagoras established that to be the first erudition which subsists through music, and also through certain melodies and rhythms, from which the remedies of human manners and passions are obtained, together with those harmonies of the powers of the soul which it possessed from the first... For Pythagoras was of the opinion that music contributed greatly to health, if it was used in an appropriate manner. He was accustomed to employ a purification of this kind, but not in a careless way. And he called the medicine which is obtained through music by the name of purification. He likewise devised medicines calculated to repress and expel the diseases both of bodies and of souls...

(He) arranged and adapted for his disciples what are called apparatus and contrectations, divinely contriving mixtures of certain diatonic, chromatic and enharmonic melodies, through which he easily transferred and circularly led the passions of the soul into a contrary direction when they had recently and in an irrational and clandestine manner been formed; such as sorrow, rage, pity, appetites, pride, supineness and vehemence. For he corrected each of these by the rule of virtue, tempering them through appropriate melodies, as through certain salutary medicines.

In the evening, likewise, when his disciples were retiring to sleep, he liberated them by certain odes and peculiar songs from diurnal perturbations and tumults, and purified their intellective power from the influxive and effluxive waves of a corporeal nature, rendered their sleep quiet, and their dreams pleasing and prophetic. But when they again rose from their beds he freed them from nocturnal heaviness, relaxation and torpor, through certain peculiar songs and modulations produced either by simply striking the lyre or employing the voice.

Pythagoras, however, did not procure for himself a thing of this kind through instruments or the voice, but, employing a certain ineffable divinity which it is difficult to apprehend, he extended his ears and fixed his intellect in the sublime symphonies of the world, he alone hearing and understanding, as it appears, the universal harmony and consonance of the spheres and the stars that are moved through them and which produce a fuller and more intense melody than anything effected by mortal sounds. This melody also was the result of dissimilar and variously differing sounds, celerities, magnitudes and intervals arranged with reference to each other in a certain most musical ratio, and thus producing a most gentle and at the same time variously beautiful motion and convolution. Being therefore irrigated, as it were, with this melody, having the reason of his intellect well arranged through it and, as I may say, exercised, he determined to exhibit certain images of these things to his disciples as much as possible, especially producing an imitation of them through instruments and through the mere voice alone.

Sometimes also, by musical sounds alone, unaccompanied with words, they (the Pythagoreans) healed the passions of the soul and certain diseases, enchanting, as they say, in reality. And it is probable that from hence this name epode, i.e., enchantment, came to be generally used.'

Pythagoras's approach sounds remarkably similar to the contemporary use of meditation music, especially if Henry Sigerist is correct in his evaluation that the ancient Greeks regarded music as 'a kind of psychotherapy that affected the body through the medium of the soul.' As Sigerist writes in *Civilisation and Disease*, 'When a disorder had developed, the Greek physician tried to restore the lost balance physically with medicine, mentally with music...'*

There is nothing strange about this when one relates the idea to modern trends. Many contemporary practitioners of holistic health-care employ music as a part of their therapy, and this serves as a powerful reminder that few ideas are really new. The current interest in meditation music is thus a contemporary revival of an old idea.

Nevertheless, some writers – among them Peter Michael Hamel – are sceptical about the value and concept of 'meditation music'. In *Through Music to the Self* Hamel asks: does it even exist? 'If one knows how to meditate, and has the necessary patience to press forward into deep inner levels, one listens inwardly and exterior sources of sound are scarcely perceived at all.' However he agrees that music 'can provide a meditative point of departure' and 'can also serve as an aid and a tool for relaxation, concentration and the achievement of inner quietness.'**

The noted astrologer and musician Dane Rudhyar has no doubt at all, however, that meditation music can 'relax taut nerves and induce quasi-hypnotic states in which the mind may become quiet as a lake reflecting the sky.' In his book *The Magic of Tone and the Art of Music* he places the issue clearly in context. For him the increasing interest in meditation music reflects the desire of many people, especially the younger generation, to return to a more natural lifestyle:

'The generation that has expressed itself in the many experiments of avant-garde music also has expressed its yearning for a return to both nature and simplicity... In music, the desire for simplicity and the longing to return to a life sustained and inspired by the experience of primordial natural energies, has taken the form of "minimal music". This music features the constant repetition of simple sequences of sounds linked by harmonic relationships.'***

**H. Sigerist: 1962 p. 149 **P.M. Hamel: 1976 p. 141 ***Dane Rudhyar: 1982, p. 113*

Other writers, including those working in a more orthodox therapeutic context, have provided insights into the nature of healing music. Dr Sydney Mitchell, quoted in the proceedings of the Royal Medical Association, believes that 'impressionist music, that is music of a sensuous fluid character, enables the listener to drift along with the music and gives greater opportunities for deep seated ideas to come to the surface.'*

When Dr Mitchell expressed these opinions in 1951 the meditation music genre as such did not exist. But what a lyrical and accurate description it provides of the style we now call 'new age', 'relaxation' or 'meditation' music!

Juliette Alvin also believes that this type of music is profoundly effective in its practical applications. She writes:

'It often is the dreamy, non-emotional, sensuous quality of music that penetrates without provoking the patient's resistance to more potent music. Moreover, sensuous melodic music has a physically relaxing effect and helps towards relaxation. It makes no emotional or dynamic demands on the listener.'**

These words, too, were written over a decade ago, and yet they reflect the more recent interest in creating music for enhancing inner states of awareness. As we will see in a later chapter, the rise of New Age music – of which meditation music is a part – dates from around 1975 and was born of necessity, for the busy and frantic world had evoked it into being as a natural response to life in the fast lane. And why not? As Bhagwan Shree Rajneesh once said: 'If your body and soul are balanced, you will attain to the greatest music possible.'

---

* *Juliette Alvin: 1975, p. 141* ** *Ibid, p. 141*

2 THE HOLISTIC APPROACH TO HEALTH

Despite the fact that this book is primarily about music and visualisation, our basic underlying focus is on holistic well-being, because this, for us, is what 'healing' really means. So, it is perhaps appropriate to outline first what we mean by the holistic approach.

For some readers it may seem overly simplistic to talk in terms of 'health for body, mind and spirit', but that – in essence – is what the philosophy of holistic healthcare is all about. There are, however, various consequences of thinking this way, which differentiate the holistic approach from the more traditional perspectives of contemporary western medicine.

Here, in a nutshell, are some of the general characteristics of mainstream orthodox healthcare:

- Health is perceived largely in terms of the absence of disease and attention is placed on treating the specific symptom or body part which has gone wrong.
- The framework of reference is substantially physical, since body effects are easier to measure than moods, emotions and feelings. Stress is, admittedly, acknowledged by some doctors as an underlying cause of disease but the focus is on treating physical symptoms of disease as they appear.
- Western medicine is, for the most part, curative rather than preventive.
- Particular medicines are recommended as treatments for specific disease states on a general, all-encompassing basis (e.g. aspirin for headache). Treatments are not usually tailored to individual requirements but are prescribed for a given condition.
- Most western doctors pay little attention to the social context of the patient: they treat the illness rather than the person.
- Patients are not given responsibility for their own health but are provided with prescriptions or treatments which place them in a position of dependence on the doctor.
- Illness is generally regarded as a complaint to be eliminated rather than a condition which can, in itself, provide insights and opportunities for self-discovery.
- Western medicine is becoming increasingly technological and scientific. Complex medical treatments are assumed to be more accurate and relevant than simpler techniques of diagnosis.
- Health is seen as a state only obtained and maintained by on-going medical attention, rather than by self-help.

– There is more emphasis on the vulnerability of human-beings to disease than on the intrinsic durability and resilience of the human organism.

Much of this comes down to the point that in modern western society we have been subtly programmed by our cultural norms not to depend overly on our own resources, and as a consequence we somehow believe in ourselves less. The philosophy of holistic health – health for the whole person – seeks to redress this tendency.

The term 'holism' was first used in the modern context in 1928 by the South African philosopher Jan Smuts in his book *Holism and Evolution.* However, as the word itself suggests, the term is much older than this. *Holos* is the ancient Greek word for 'whole' and from it we derive our English expressions 'holy', 'whole', 'health' and even the greeting 'hello'. Plato was an advocate of the holistic approach to well-being, and we have this quotation from him:

'The cure of the part should not be attempted without treatment of the whole. No attempts should be made to cure the body without the soul, and if the head and body are to be healthy you must begin by curing the mind, for this is the great error of our day in the treatment of the human body, that physicians first separate the soul from the body.'

Fortunately, there are doctors and healthcare professionals who are beginning to apply the Platonic philosophy in the modern context. In *Dimensions of Humanistic Medicine*, a modern treatise on holistic medicine, the authors make an appeal for a return to a broader vision of mankind:

'A person is more than his body. Every human being is a holistic, interdependent relationship of body, emotions, mind and spirit. The clinical process which causes the patient to consult the medical profession is best understood as this whole and dynamic relationship. The maintenance of continued health depends on harmony of this whole.'*

So what are the broad characteristics of *holistic* healthcare, as distinct from the more traditional medical perspectives outlined earlier?

Taking the previous list and itemising each point by way of comparison, we can make the following contrasts:

In the holistic approach –

– Health is seen as a positive and natural state and is conceived in terms of the whole being of the patient, not in terms of rectifying a particular isolated symptom.

– The framework of reference is much broader that the purely physical. It encom-

*S. Miller *Dimensions of Humanistic Medicine*, quoted in K. Pelletier: 1979, p 35

passes the mental and emotional aspects of health and also such areas as spiritual values, the search for personal meaning, and the integrative nature of religious beliefs. Stress is considered to be a state of imbalance between parts of the organism in relation to the whole.

– The focus is more on prevention than cure. This brings with it an emphasis on such self-help factors as sensible nutrition, exercise and personal involvement in preventing the onset of disease. Where cures *are* required, treatments will not be simply for symptoms but for balance, integration and total well-being.

– The patient is encouraged to take responsibility for his state of health and to be as self-reliant as possible. The emphasis is on the positive promotion of health and the prevention of disease.

– Illness may be perceived as providing the opportunity for personal growth and self-discovery. One learns to question why a condition of imbalance has arisen and to seek ways of rectifying personal deficiencies which may have contributed to such disease states. This is particularly true in the case of holistic treatments for cancer where emotional or lifestyle imbalances are isolated as a cause of stress, contributing to breakdowns in the immune system and the outbreak of tumours. Similarly, nutritional factors such as excessive intake of saturated fats, may be perceived as contributing to coronary heart disease, and a new and more balanced lifestyle adopted as a consequence.

– Respect is paid to traditional systems of healthcare like acupuncture, herbalism, aruyvedic medicine, homeopathy and yoga, as well as to the advances of modern scientific medicine. The earlier modalities are perceived as having value as 'complementary' styles of medicine, and as being useful adjuncts to modern science. Holistic therapists have no inherent problem in utilising systems not fully understood within the western scientific paradigm (this is especially true of acupuncture meridians, which are not recognised as energy channels by orthodox medicine, and also of homeopathic remedies which are extremely dilute and appear to contradict Avogadro's Law).

– The patient is encouraged not to become dependent on the doctor but to take increasing control of his own situation.

– The emphasis is placed on the remarkable capacity of the human organism to rectify imbalance and engage in a self-healing process. Natural modalities stimulate healing processes from within the organism wherever possible, rather than introduce an external agent that is 'alien'. This means that healing is as non-intrusive as possible, and does not involve chemical drugs or other 'unnatural' agents.

The holistic approach to health is a comparatively recent development in modern medicine and has emerged largely as a response to the awareness of stress as an underlying cause of disease.

One of the leading advocates of holistic lifestyles is Dr Kenneth Pelletier of the University of California School of Medicine in San Francisco. Dr Pelletier argues in his book *Mind as Healer, Mind as Slayer* that stress is necessary for most forms of positive activity but in western society this has become excessive and self-destructive. The models of behaviour most admired in our society now involve high stress levels – focusing on personal ambition, goal orientation, financial prosperity – and this means that we all have to learn how to cope with stress more efficiently.

For executives and others subject to lifestyle pressures this means heeding such signs of stress reactions as trembling, cold feet, chills up and down the spine, a racing heart, and other such symptoms as dilated pupils, a tight throat, shallow respiration, a locked diaphragm and a rigid pelvis. It also involves recognising the fact that because most of us cannot easily escape from stress we may then tend to internalise our fears, anxieties and worries. Under stress, the body produces what has become known as the 'fight-or-flight' syndrome. The heart races, body temperature rises, oxygen consumption increases – in short, the body is overtaxed. And when the body-machine is overworked the weakest part breaks first. Illness to which we are genetically, environmentally or pharmaceutically susceptible is the logical consequence.

Part of the approach in holistic counselling is to try to isolate stressors in one's lifestyle – that is to say, specific stress-causing agents – and eliminate them systematically. These changes may range from a relatively minor problem, like modifying caffeine-overload, to balancing family and work commitments or practising techniques of stress-control like meditation. The larger part of this book deals with methods of stress reduction featuring meditation and relaxation music. However, at this point it is worth noting that during meditation various physical changes occur. The rate of breathing and heart-beat become slower, less oxygen is consumed, blood pressure goes down and stabilises, skin conductivity decreases and there is an enhanced sence of personal meaning and well-being. In short, meditation is good for your health.

It used to be said by critics of holistic healthcare that such 'alternative' thinking was simply mysticism and make-believe. How could such things as meditation and visualisation affect the workings of the body? What exactly were the mechanisms?

Some of the answers are now being provided by a new science – psychoneuroimmunology (PNI).

Basically, PNI researchers are now involved in the intriguing task of investigating how the brain interacts with the body's immune cells – how the brain sends signals via the nerves to enable the body to fight disease. Since these pathways can be triggered by thoughts and emotions, such research is useful for discovering how seemingly subjective or intangible holistic therapies are in fact working with something physiologically real.

The new finding is that the brain and immune system constitute a closed circuit and that there is a two-way interaction between the immune system and the brain which monitors the presence of intrusive bacteria, tumours and viruses in the body.

Neuropharmacologist Dr Candace Pert, who works for the National Institute of Mental Health in the United States, believes that neuropeptides – small protein-like chemicals made in the brain – operate rather like 'biochemical units of emotion'. The neuropeptides, which include the well-known category of endorphins, are morphine-like chemicals generated in the brain, which produce marked changes in mood. However, it also appears that neuropeptides can connect with macrophages (cells which help destroy infection and disease), influencing the speed and direction of their movement. The interaction of these two classes of chemicals in the body appears to offer a scientific explanation for an effect we all acknowledge intuitively – that our moods and state of mind can affect our state of health. For example, it may be the sheer emotional power of optimism and positive thinking which helps some people recover from seemingly 'terminal' types of illness. The reason for this is that the positive attitude itself helps to keep the immune system fighting.

Another, and more specific, insight into how holistic visualisation could work is provided by French researcher Gerard Renoux of the University of Tours. Renoux notes that in controlling the immune system, the brain requires co-operation between the left and right hemispheres of the brain. If there is a situation of altered symmetry, the delicate regulation of the immune system may become interrupted and the person becomes more vulnerable to disease. In the case of therapies involving visualisation to fight illness, the imagery itself is controlled substantially by the right side of the brain and exercises which stimulate this type of activity may help to 'distract' the brain from suppressing the immune system. At the same time, the sense of positiveness and optimism helps to stimulate the left hemisphere of the brain and insodoing strengthens the immune system's response against disease.

In other words, visualisation can be a really effective therapeutic tool in bridging brain hemisphere imbalance and maximising the body's potential for regaining a state of health and well-being.

A similar type of finding emerged recently from research at the Medical Illness Counseling Center in Chevy Chase, Maryland. There, immunologist Nick Hall and psychologists Barry Gruber and Stephen Hersh were able to demonstrate clinically that relaxation and positive mental imagery stimulated the production of lymphocytes to fight cancer tumours more effectively, thus confirming the pioneering work of such therapists as Dr Carl Simonton and Dr Laurence Le Shan, who have for several years insisted that visualisation is a vital key to recovery from cancer and other degenerative disease conditions.

Professor Ed Blalock of the University of Texas sums it up very succinctly. In a recent interview he made this point:

'Your classical sensory systems recognise things you can see, taste, touch, smell and hear. Bacteria and viruses have none of these qualities, so how are you going to know they're there unless the immune system lets your brain in on the secret?... The immune system may be the sixth sense we've been seeking all these years.'*

Holism and Music

What implications does the holistic perspective have for music? There are several general points which can be made, and also certain specifics – which we will come to later.

Of a general nature, the sort of music we are calling 'healing music' needs to be able to generate the relaxation response, or to be suitable for visualisation, guided imagery or meditation. It is music which should be potentially able to harmonise left and right brain hemisphere activity, and to stimulate integrative levels of awareness relating to body, mind and spirit. It should also be music which engages us creatively – music in which we participate as individuals without feeling swamped or dominated.

It should be music which helps us feel good about ourselves and which enables us to dig into the resources of our unconscious minds, where fears and anxieties may lie hidden. And, above all, it should be music which resonates with our whole being.

Later in this book we will describe in detail how such music – New Age music, meditation music, inner space music, call it what you will – has evolved.

Meanwhile, it is interesting to examine some of the varied research perspectives which have emerged in recent years specifically in relation to the three areas we are addressing in holism: body, mind and spirit.

Body Music

Some therapists, among them Dr John Diamond, Dr Louis Savary and Dr Steven Halpern, believe that certain sorts of music have a specific detrimental impact on the body, quite apart from perceptual reactions to the music. In Dr Diamond's words, 'we "hear" not only with our ears, but also with our bodies.'

Dr Diamond is an advocate of behavioural kinesiology and uses the well-known

*'*A New Prescription': Mind over Malady,* Discover, *February 1987, p. 59*

technique of testing the deltoid muscle to demonstrate muscle weakness. For example, Dr Diamond makes the interesting observation that most people test 'weak' when the isolated note C is played.

According to Dr Diamond the indicator muscle will test 'strong' if 'good' music is played to the subject – even if the ears are blocked with pillows or sound-absorbing material – and this demonstrates that the body can discriminate between beneficial and detrimental sounds. Dr Diamond is particularly critical of heavy rock music from groups like Queen and Led Zeppelin (not so the more melodic Beatles, of whom he approves) and clearly favours classical music. In supporting his argument he notes that orchestral conductors as remarkably long-lived – presumably because they are surrounded by life-enhancing music.

'The average age of death of the American male is 68.9 years' says Dr Diamond, 'yet at 70, some 80 percent of conductors are still alive and working.' At the time he published his book (1979) Pablo Casals – aged 96 – headed the list of active musical conductors, followed by Rudolph Ganz and Leopold Stokowski, both aged 95.

On another level, of course, the body responds to music because of the biological correlations between pulse and rhythm. As we mentioned earlier, the basic facets of our existence – breathing, running, walking, the pulse of the heart – are rhythmic and our response to musical rhythm reflects this. In the same way that a voodoo dancer loses consciousness in the overwhelming tide of sound which pours from a frantic tirade of drums at a pace far beyond the tempo of normal biological rhythm – so too meditation music features gentle, undulating rhythms which are slow and relaxing. And there is undoubtedly a physiological reason for this, as Drs Halpern and Savary point out in *Sound Health*. Quoting *Science News* (April 24: 1984), they note that scientists have discovered that DNA molecules oscillate in resonance in microwaves. 'Is it not possible' they ask, 'that musical vibrations, made by musical instruments or our own voices, can have an effect on how the cells of our body are arranged?'

It is all a matter of sympathetic vibration...

Mind Music

As we have seen, music provides a direct channel to the emotions and stimulates the intuitive, right-hemisphere side of the brain. Dr Helen Bonny of the Institute for Consciousness and Music in the United States takes a similar view to Dr Diamond's, and has utilised the music of several prominent classical composers – including Bach, Haydn, Vivaldi, Debussy and Bizet – in stress-reduction programmes for hospital patients. Her *Music Rx* programmes of taped music were tested in the intensive care units of Jefferson General Hospital, Washington, and St Agnes Hospital, Baltimore, over two six-month periods, and demonstrated that the 'quieting of mood state' induced by the music brought with it a 'measurable reduction of heart rate in patients after listening to music programmes. Psychological ratings showed positive effects on depression and anxiety as well as relief of pain.'

If we consider the holistic model, it makes sense that a state of creative well-being involves the equal participation of both hemispheres of the brain. Music stimulates imagination, intuition and creativity – all aspects of the right hemisphere – and can therefore help complement the dominant left-hemisphere functions which characterise western intellectual behaviour patterns. As Dr Diamond writes in *Life Energy*:

'It is the synthesis of the functions of the hemispheres that leads to true understanding. That is what great poetry, great music, all great art forms, through the use of metaphor, can initiate for us – true comprehension, perception, knowing. The whole of "logic" and "intuition" is so much more than merely the sum of its parts. The two streams of the brain meet in a tremendous outburst of creativity.'*

The impact of music on the emotions, of course, has long been of interest to musicologists and therapists and as long ago as 1937, in *The American Journal of Psychology*, Kate Hevner suggested an eight-fold classification of music and poetry in terms of mood response. Her eight elements were:

– solemn and sacred
– sad and doleful
– tender and sentimental
– quiet and soothing
– sprightly and playful
– gay and happy
– exhilarated and exciting
– vigorous and majestic

This is, of course, a purely individual response to the division of moods, and other variants are possible. However, the essential point is this: since music is an ideal medium for stimulating visual imagery there is an obvious benefit in choosing selections of recorded music as a background for specific therapeutic functions, ranging from stimulation through to relaxation and meditation, and they encompass such mood states as those listed above. In our aggressive and highly stress-inducing culture it is, however, the gentler and more soothing range of music which is of most interest to us here, and which occupies the main focus of the latter part of this book.

**John Diamond: 1986 p. 87*

Spirit Music

In recent times two frameworks have been proposed for classifying the consciousness-expanding qualities of New Age music: the 'chakra' system of Dr Steven Halpern and 'classification by the elements' suggested by the co-author of the present volume, Nevill Drury. Both are attempts to evaluate the use of music not only in relation to the functions of mind and body, but also of the spirit. What we are calling 'spirit' is, of course, highly intangible and means different things to different people. However, within the paradigm of health we are presenting here, it represents what many holistic therapists consider to be the very ground of our being – the true basis of our existence. It is characterised not by the language of scientific analysis but by poetic metaphor and symbols of transcendence – motifs which point the way to the sacred and Infinite.

American therapist Dr Steven Halpern – himself a New Age musician and a scholar of musical forms – has adopted a framework which utilises the concept of the chakras and Kundalini. The latter represents a system of energy levels in yoga but Dr Halpern modified it to correlate with notes on the musical scale and the 'rainbow' colours of the spectrum. His correlations, presented in his books *Tuning the Human Instrument*, and *Sound Health* look like this:

Note	*Colour*	*Kundalini Chakra*
C	Red	Muladhara
D	Orange	Svadisthana
E	Yellow	Manipura
F	Green	Anahata
G	Blue	Visuddha
A	Indigo	Ajna
B	Violet	Sahasrara

Halpern's system is symbolically appealing to the extent that the base chakras of *Muladhara* and *Svadisthana* correlate with the dynamic segments of the spectrum and the energy levels progress musically to the more transcendent reaches of consciousness associated with *Ajna* and *Sahasrara* and the meditative colours of indigo and violet.

A problem with Halpern's system, however, is that the colours do not equate with the traditional symbolic colours ascribed by the Hindus themselves to these chakras. Nevertheless, the point is made that one can progress meditatively from the active energy levels to the more introspective realms of spiritual awareness using these musical scales.

Nevill Drury's framework, outlined in the recently published *Music for Inner Space*, places emphasis not on a spectrum of colours so much as on the five elements which are central to a number of metaphysical systems – including yoga, astrology, tarot and western alchemical mysticism. These elements, again in order from lowest to highest are:

Earth (level of everyday consciousness)
Water
Fire
Air
Spirit (transcendental awareness)

In this system, New Age music is divided into categories based on personal association – Earth-music, Water-music, Fire-music, and so on – and meditators select recorded music to enhance their ambient visualisations. Of necessity, this is a highly individual choice, but lists of recorded music are presented in the latter part of this book to provide a starting point for the development of a personal collection of meditative music (see Appendix). The key emphasis is that music should be tested by the individual meditator to ensure that it evokes specific associations. If the music and the visualisation are competing against each other in terms of affective response, the value of the combination is obviously diminished. At all times the music is useful only as a specific and enhancing meditative point of departure. What is of special interest here is that, in practical terms, selections for the element Spirit are usually suitable as generalised ambient backgrounds for relaxation and meditation. Such music is typically devoid of strong melodic content, leads us into a state of mind expansion, but nevertheless remains gentle and reflective in quality. It is music which literally enhances our inner journey of the spirit.

3 THE ENERGY LEVELS WITHIN

Life's music never stops –
we are constantly playing on it,
with it and in it.

Timothy Kelly

Sound is our constant companion. From our first moment of awareness in the womb we swim in a sea of sound. Our reality is aligned to the rhythmic beating of our mother's heart and the tidal flow of her body fluids. Beyond these immediate melodies we are aware of the muffled input from an outer reality. The events occurring around her are toned down and filtered before they reach us, but because they affect her emotionally we begin to feel them as deeply as she does. Sounds that bring fear to her are similarly anchored in ourselves, and we too will trigger to those sounds in later life.

As we develop, the sounds of our own body begin to flow in rhythm with those of our mother. We draw our security from these familiar sounds of 'home'. This is our whole world, our universe. Imagine then the intense shock of going through the painful birth process and emerging into an unfamiliar world where our security blanket of familiar sounds is no longer there, and noise invades our very being. Our protective layer against the things that happen out there has suddenly been ripped from us and we lie naked and exposed. Sounds that in the womb had been faint or very distant are now terrifyingly close and invasive. Every sense in our body is thrown into confusion and we begin this life by being thrown off-centre.

The human body is, however, a masterly creation and soon adapts to the new levels of input. Before long what was at first an invasive force now becomes the familiar.

For example, a child who has become used to loud sounds in its environment becomes frightened when faced with the silence of the nursery. Similarly a child conditioned to rural life is overwhelmed by the sounds of the city.

Begin to recall familiar sounds from your own childhood. Perhaps you can still hear the invasion of the school bell and the cacophony of noise in the playground.

As we grow up to the raucous clatter of modern life in the West, noise is a constant invasion tending to throw us off-centre and out of tune with our natural rhythm. It is common knowledge that most industrial accidents occur in areas of high noise pollution.

We are constantly amazed at how well our bodies adapt to the environment. Most of us can recall a time when we have had to move into a noisy environment for a prolonged period of time. At first we would have been very aware of the noise levels and probably very uncomfortable with them. Yet in a matter of hours or sometimes days we have become so accustomed to the noise levels that they become no more than background rumblings. It is only when these background rumblings stop for some reason that we notice that they are not there. Any city dweller who has been taken out into the countryside for some time will invariably experience difficulty sleeping on the first night out. The country is too quiet. The familiar background noises are no longer there and the individual is disturbed by the lack of the familiar sounds. After some time in the country the peace and quiet then becomes familiar and so when returning to the cities these people will probably have a few disturbed nights while they readjust to what is to be their new familiar background.

The problem we experience with the external clatter is that it tends to overpower our internal rhythms leading to confusion and even muscle weakness. As mentioned earlier, this has been clearly demonstrated by Dr John Diamond's work in behavioural kinesiology. The effect of high level noise or sudden disturbing noise is most readily witnessed in psychiatric institutions. It only takes one person to react in a loud way to set the whole group catharting and we can see the reflection of that in society in general when we realise that at least one percent of the total population is suffering from some form of schizophrenia. This percentage is on the increase in line with expanding industrialisation and noise pollution.

An experiment was recently conducted on national television to demonstrate the effect of noise levels on mood changes. The television crew staged a scene when an elderly lady walking along a busy sidewalk dropped her bag of shopping. Without hesitation several fellow pedestrians immediately stopped and helped her reclaim her scattered goods. Having filmed the sequence they then brought in a work crew with jack hammers and began noisily to dig up the road at this point. With the noise in progress they then restaged the scene. The elderly lady once again dropped her bag of shopping only this time nobody stopped to help her. The noise levels had obviously closed the other pedestrians off to their feelings towards her. Noise has the effect of making people less sympathetic and results in increased aggression and anger responses.

Sound can be both constructive and destructive. The body responds to some forms of sound in a similar way as it does to food. It can use these sounds as a source of food and nourishment. You only have to sit back and listen to a full rendering of Pachelbel's *Canon* or Beethoven's *Pastorale Symphony* to feel the sense of warmth and fullness within. The crystal calling of a bird at dawn can have the same effect. Ancient cultures found it very important to spend time with Nature and atuning to the earth.

While in the womb we align ourselves to the vibration of our mother. Once out in the world we need to align ourselves to a similar vibration and can readily identify with the earth as the mother force. For those of you who have read the works of Sir Laurence van der Post you will undoubtedly have felt the heartbeat and pulse of Africa. It is to this pulsation that we lean in search of mother. As Pythagoras stated in his early works 'All things are constructed on harmonic patterns'. It is only when we are out of step with the natural harmonic that disharmony arises. Living our lives in the fast lane of western society we have lost touch with our basic natural rhythms. How more important therefore is it for us to find the time and space for attunement and balance as did our forefathers. One of the best and most accessible ways of doing this in our technological age is through the use of healing music.

In therapeutic situations healing, or ambient music has the ability to detour around the ego and mind, and is thus able to stir up latent conflicts and emotions. The initial use of familiar melodies, especially if they are repeated over and over, tends to relax and open the client allowing them to be more receptive to the unconscious blocks that may be presented. Directed or specific sounds may then help to explore the levels of consciousness not normally available to the person. The renowned Italian psychologist Dr Roberto Assagioli has given us a simple but dramatic illustration of these various unconscious levels of the psyche in what is commonly referred to as his 'egg diagram'.

(DIAGRAM 1)

1. Lower unconscious
2. Middle unconscious
3. Higher unconscious or superconscious
4. Field of consciousness
5. Personal self or 'I'
6. Transpersonal self
7. Collective unconscious

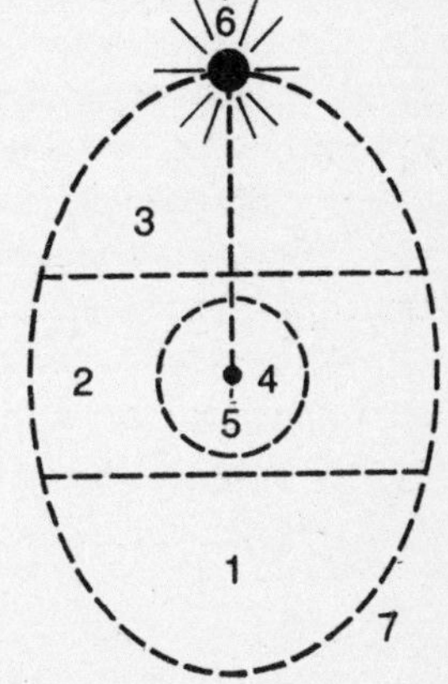

All lines in the diagram are represented by dots symbolising a constant interplay between all demarcated areas. In other words, nothing survives in isolation. Everything is connected and has an effect on everything else. Referring to the diagram, we have three basic areas of the psyche. These are the lower unconscious (1) which mainly represents our personal psychological past in the form of repressed complexes, memories and drives. The middle unconscious (2) represents the consciousness that is available to us but not necessarily 'in mind' at any one moment. The upper section of the diagram represents the higher unconscious (3) and is the fertile field of inspiration and intuition. This is also the source of our higher feelings such as altruistic love, humanitarianism and heroic action. At the centre of the egg is the personal self or 'I' (5) and is representative of the way we see ourselves as a personality. Around the personal self lies our immediate field of consciousness (4), the field of which we are aware at any one moment. If you were asked to recall the telephone number in the house in which you lived as a child, you might have initial difficulty in finding the answer. The number would not be in the immediate field of consciousness but would lie in the middle unconscious (2) and be accessible to us were we to put our mind to the task. Shining like a bright star is the transpersonal self, (6), or higher self and is in effect our guiding light or soul. And surrounding the whole of the egg is what Jung termed the Collective Unconscious, which he described as 'The precondition of each individual psyche, just as the sea is the carrier of each individual wave'. The Collective Unconscious is, in effect, the mass experience of all humanity.

Looking at the above diagram one can see how limited we are in our everyday consciousness. By the use of sound in various forms of ambient music we are not only able to extend our field of consciousness to embrace the middle unconscious, but also to elicit information from lower and higher unconscious states. Mozart, for example, was not a genius in the accepted sense of the word. A genius like Einstein would have the field of consciousness (4) expanded to overlap into higher and lower unconscious levels at all times giving him virtually free access to these realms. Mozart was in fact rather simple, but had the ability to access information, in his case music, from the higher unconscious almost as though somebody else was writing the music through him. Our field of consciousness is very much limited by the left hemisphere or rational brain. It is only when we make the connection to the right hemisphere through music and the arts that we can begin to expand our consciousness to include all states. Healing music stimulates our natural curiosity and creativity which in turn will naturally lead us to states of higher consciousness.

So how can energy in the form of sound have such a marked effect on us?

Energy underlies every cell and every atom of our being. It is energy that in essence holds us together. Remove the energy component from our bodies and we would end up as no more than a pool of water on the floor containing various chemicals and trace elements. As a basic model begin to imagine a cylinder of energy pulsating towards a central axis. This central axis in effect becomes the spine, and attracts around it the physical matter of the body. The cylinder effect, however, extends way beyond what we have amassed as a physical body. With this model you will begin to understand the importance of the energy component of our presence here. Around the body, and in fact around all living things, lies an energy field which we term the aura. This aura is composed of seven different layers of energy, becoming more subtle the further you move out from the body.

In practical terms it is important for us to consider the innermost five levels as they relate directly to the way we function in the world. The innermost level, which is effective from the centre of the spine to about two inches beyond the physical, is known as the etheric and is in effect our pre-physical body. Stretching from the spine outwards to about eight inches from the physical lies the astral body which deals with our emotional states. Extending beyond that we come to the lower mental body, which is very much a left-hemisphere or rational mind function, and then to the upper mental which is more the right-hemisphere function or the intuitive. The fifth level, which extends as far as our outreached fingertips, we refer to as the spiritual level – not, however, in a 'church' sense but rather in a sense of why we are here, or the purpose of our life. These auras have for some years been photographed in colour by Kirlian photography. Kirlian photography has demonstrated very clearly the sense of energy underlying all physical matter. In early experiments researchers photographed a freshly picked leaf and found around the leaf an aura of energy. They then cut a large segment from the leaf and photographed the remainder once more. What they discovered there, was that the photograph clearly showed the disfigured leaf surrounded by the still complete aura. In other words taking away physical matter had no effect on the underlying energy pattern. Some of you will have heard stories about people who have had a limb amputated and are still bothered by an itchy sensation in the extremity. Although the leg had been removed the toes still itch in their energy form!

Kirlian photography was then developed to handle the emanation from larger objects and various experiments were conducted around the effective use of energy through the body. One of the first of these experiments was to photograph the hand of a healer while at rest. The energy pattern obtained was no different than from a hundred other hands. The healer then began to transmit energy through the hand and the resultant picture showed a massive increase in the size and intensity of the emanations. Kirlian photography has now been taken to the point where skilled technicians can diagnose the state of health or disease of a person by the patterning obtained on film.

Stop for a moment and consider how in touch you are with your aura. Recall the last time you were with people at a party and you felt uncomfortable with the person standing next to you. What in fact was happening here was an intermingling of your aura with the other person's aura, and your unconscious recognition that his or her aura was not conducive to yours. All you felt was a sense of discomfort, or perhaps mistrust, and the desire to move away. The same applies when you feel that somebody has 'rubbed you up the wrong way'. The feeling is purely a translation of an energy input.

Within the aura and operating at right angles to it we have numerous energy centres. In Eastern philosophy these energy centres are referred to as *chakras*, meaning 'wheels of energy'. In each human there are 1000 energy centres, and these are divided into categories of 7 major, 21 minor, 49 lesser and 923 tiny ones. In the framework of this book we will be looking briefly at the seven major centres, as it is these that have the most marked effect on our lives.

David Tansley in his book *Radionics and the Subtle Anatomy of Man* describes the chakra as being a source of power that determines the physical, emotional and mental makeup of man, and therefore is the key to health and well-being. In *Subtle-Body Healing*, Victor Beasley describes the function of the chakra as being to receive, assimilate and distribute energy or *prana*. It is the chakra that is able to convert energy into electro-chemical impulses in the body. Annie Wilson in *What Colour Are You?* concludes that our well-being depends on the correct reception and distribution of energies, and when the chakras are all evenly balanced the body is in perfect harmony with the mind, emotions and spirit. This correlates with Jung when he says, 'In the process of individuation the psyche becomes "whole" when a balance is achieved between four functions: thinking, feeling, sensing and intuiting.' Jung also equates the chakras as being 'the gateways of consciousness in man, receptive points for the inflow of energies from the cosmos and the spirit and soul of man.'

Blocked energies do not disappear. Any emotion that we have experienced at any time in our lives, and that has not been expressed, is locked into the body and remains as memories within rigidified muscular tissue and body armour. It is now possible to relocate these blocks through using the seven major chakras, and to release them with the use of physical expression and various forms of mental imagery. To access the information locked within each chakra we need a deeper understanding of the practical and philosophical aspects of the energy concerned. In the past we have relied on information from the East regarding the chakra system, yet this information had been written for a people who were very different to the modern-day inhabitants of the West. In the West we have relied on psychology and the sciences to come to terms with our role on this planet. It is our belief as co-authors that neither Eastern philosophy nor Western psychology alone contains the full picture.

Andrew Watson, co-author of the present book, has for the past 12 years been a pioneer in bringing together Eastern philosophy and Western psychology. Through his extended work with individuals as well as groups around the world he has developed a map of the chakra system that has been proven to be effective in thousands of case studies, and applicable to people living in both Eastern and Western societies. His work and research are the subject of his book *Wheels of Life* to be published in the near future.

To give you a better understanding of the energies involved we offer you the following breakdown on each of the seven major chakras to enable you to participate more fully in the following chapters. As this book is designed primarily for Western consumption we shall dispense with the Eastern terminology and use simple language.

All chakras are evident as conical energy fields in both front and back planes of the body, and reference will be given to their exact position in both these planes. Confusion still exists amongst certain seers about the exact location of each centre. Those seers who operate from an emotional base will perceive the chakra to be active only from the spine in a forward direction, whereas those who operate on a mental plane will perceive the chakra to extend backwards. It is purely a question of where you stand to perceive a particular event. We have discovered that in fact chakra energy fields extend both front and back. To every action there is an equal and opposite reaction and thus, in effect, both seers mentioned above were correct in their limited perspective.

Root Chakra

The root has to do with the qualities of survival, power and aggression and is situated at the apex of the coccyx at the rear, and on the top edge of the pubic bone on the front elevation. The root manifests in the adrenal glands and controls the spine, kidneys and skin and is part-controller of the bladder. It is directly connected to vitality and controls our 'fight and flight' response. In the root we find a basic fear – the fear of being here. This is the fear of incarnation – of being human on this plane now. The root also acts as an anchor in relation to mental stability and without this anchor the person will tend towards schizophrenia. The root acts as a channel for the will-to-be to express itself. It serves to animate the physical body. As Alice A. Bailey notes in her writings the root can be equated as a source of life to the substances of the body, and as the basis of all physical matter.

According to the state of function of this centre we are able to define four distinct character types:

Underactive The underactive root chakra would support a quiet passive person, one who is inclined to states of deep depression and who feels impotent in relation to authority. This person would tend to be caught in the role of the underdog all their life.

Overactive Here we have a person who has excess fight and aggression, a person who tends to be very proud and unbending and who loves to be in control at all times. This person would have no concept of surrender and will fight to the end.

Excess flight This category epitomises the fearful person, somebody who is always running away. They would exhibit great anxiety and possible nervous disorders. The paranoid schizoid typifies this state.

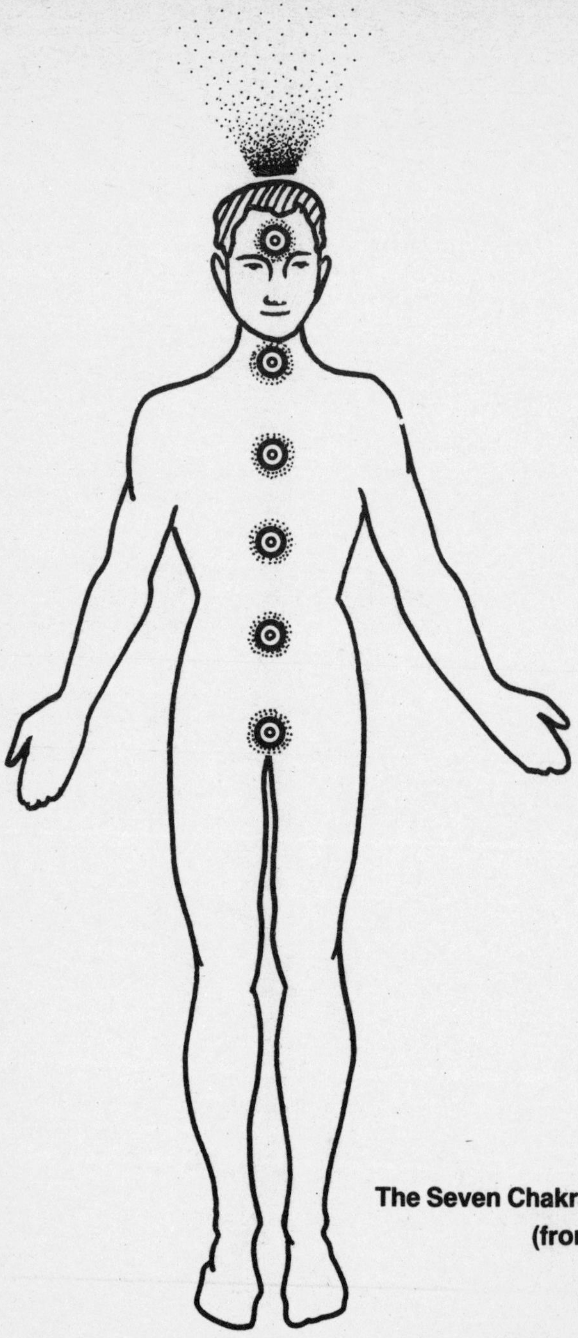

The Seven Chakras
(front)

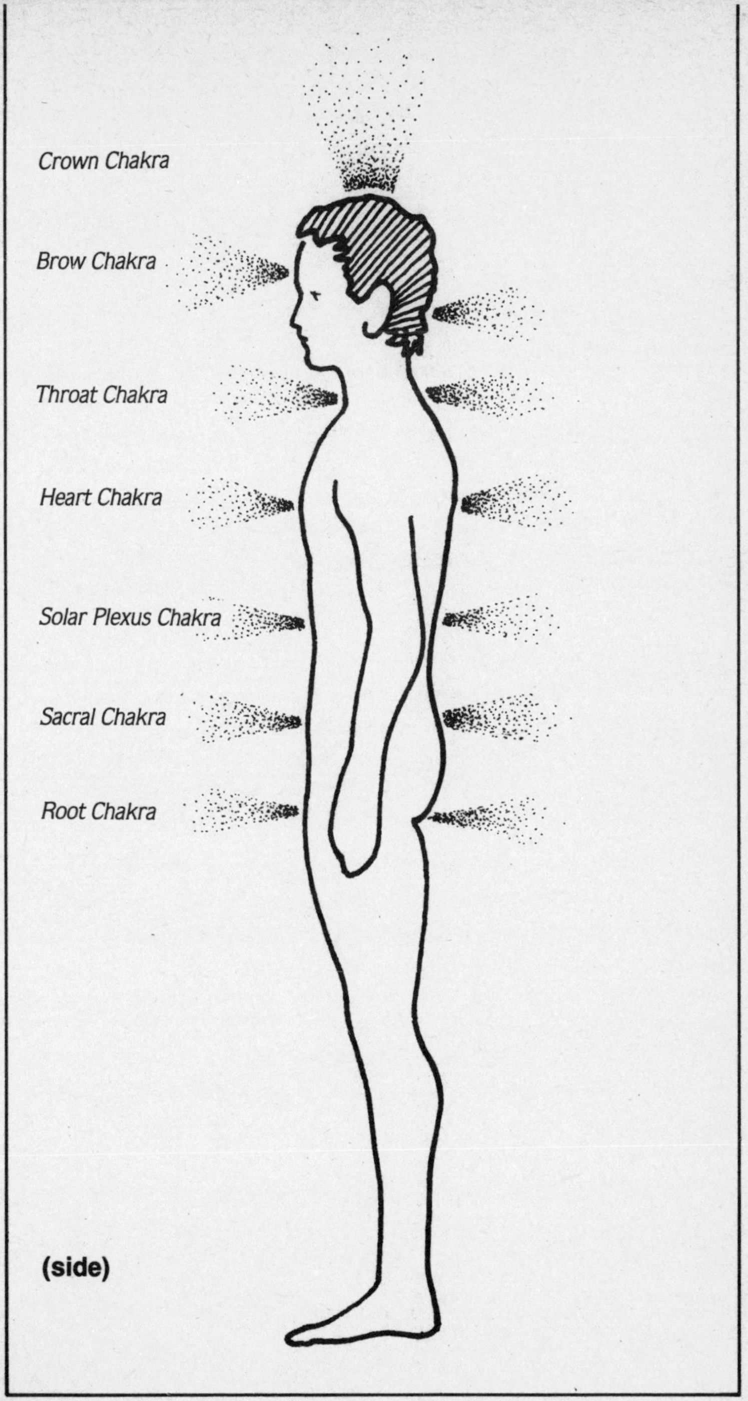

Crown Chakra

Brow Chakra

Throat Chakra

Heart Chakra

Solar Plexus Chakra

Sacral Chakra

Root Chakra

(side)

Mis-channelled In this state we find a person who is manipulative in order to get what they want. This person appears to be helpless and uses that helplessness to control everybody around them. Such people are masters in the art of passive aggression, and are often seen as the power behind the throne. In themselves they have no sense of personal direction in life, and live their lives through others.

Sacral Chakra

The sacral chakra governs the qualities of sexuality, sensuality and personal creativity. On the body it is found at the base of the lumbar spine on the back, a little over an inch below the naval on the front of the body. It controls the glands, the sex organs, potency and the fluid functions of the body. It is also half-controller of the bladder. Situated at this particular point on the spine it plays a very important role in our general well-being and uprightness. One of the most common symptoms of an imbalance in this centre is the disturbance of a woman's natural monthly cycle. Over 70 percent of women attending the author's clinic suffered some form of disturbance to the natural menstrual cycle, which is very indicative of our unbalanced lifestyle in the West. All problems related to impotence, infertility or rhythmic dysfunctions can be treated effectively in this centre.

Two basic character types are found here:

Underactive The underactive person will normally display a low sexual drive with little sense of their own worth. They tend to have strong programming from church or society around their own sexuality, and end up with a tremendous amount of guilt and shame. As the centre is connected with fluid functions, this type of person will often become dried out in later life.

Overactive Here we discover a very obsessive character who tends to attempt to gather everything around themselves. Their focus is very strongly on attachment – attachment to children, places or material possessions. Their desire is to become the owner of all they perceive.

People who have been brought up in a colonial society will undoubtedly have heard the instruction 'stomach in, chest out, shoulders back, chin up'. The military-type effect of this enforced posture is to block off all feeling in the pelvis, to suppress hormonal function and to repress personal power and expression. We can be thankful that the 'stiff upper lip' era is now passing.

Solar Plexus Chakra

The solar plexus is the seat of the emotions and deeper feelings, and is said to be the clearing house of all the lower energies in the system. It is found where the concave lumbar spine straightens out before flowing into the convex thoracic spine. On the front of the body it is positioned where the ribs divide at the base of the sternum. This centre manifests in the pancreas gland and controls the liver, gall bladder, stomach and intestines. It would seem to be the seat of nervous disorders, and is often held responsible for skin eruptions. Emotional repression in this centre is the major contributing factor in degenerative diseases such as cancer, heart conditions and arthritis. The solar plexus is the centre of attachment. It is here we experience one form of love – a love that says 'I love you because you make me feel good' or 'I love you because you support me in what I do'. This form of love needs a return. It has an expectation and is never given freely.

Within the solar plexus chakra we find three character types:

Underactive The person here would be typified by the absent-minded professor. A person with a near total mental polarisation who is emotionally dry, leads a very flat existence, and has great difficulty in relating to people.

Rationalised The rationalised person has a very strong mental influence on their feelings. They tend to hold themselves in a superior fashion, and become very judgmental. Rather than speak about themselves they refer to the classical 'one'. One should do this, one should be seen in a certain way, and so on.

Overactive Here we find a person with feelings which seem to oscillate like a pendulum. One moment they are on top of the world, the next in the depths of depression. They tend to have a very distorted perception of life and events around them. They have very immediate emotional needs, however, and are strongly identified with meeting these needs – often at the cost of those around them.

Heart Chakra

The qualities associated with the heart centre are unconditional love, impersonal feelings and concepts of the whole or group consciousness. The heart is found midway between the shoulder blades on the spine and centred on the sternum. This centre manifests in the thymus gland and controls the heart, the blood circulation and most importantly the immune system. It is therefore possible that the answer to the AIDS epidemic will be found in developing an unconditional love for the whole. Other aspects found in this centre are responsibility, compassion, humility, tolerance, empathy and trust.

The character types found here are:

Underactive The archetypal, hard-headed business person who seems so intolerant and amoral comes to mind. This person will be very self-protective, find it hard to trust, and probably be very irresponsible. Perhaps the unscrupulous second-hand car dealer is the most fitting example.

Overactive This type of person tends to become immersed in the problem. They are so identified with the pain of war or starvation, that they get sucked in, and become totally ineffective. How many times have you read of people flying off to help, in some drought-stricken region of Africa where starvation is prevalent? These people are so caught up in the pain of starvation and the need to help that they lose sight of the fact that by going there themselves they are creating one more mouth to feed.

It is said that an open heart centre brings great understanding and love in a universal sense. The awareness in the centre is no longer caught up with the either/or struggle, but rather focuses on both/and resolution. For example the solar plexus would say, 'You have really made a mess of that project and you are a stupid fool' while the heart would respond, 'You have tried very hard there, and perhaps if you included this as well...' It is from within this centre that we get the sense of the oneness of all life. There is no separation.

Our relationship with animals allows us to feel the love from the heart, and it has been found that a pet will increase the life expectancy of heart patients by up to five years. On the other hand, unexpressed grief has been found to lower the function of the immune system and to shorten life expectancy.

Throat Chakra

The qualities of the throat chakra are expression, creativity and production. The throat is said to be our interface with the world. On a physical plane this centre is found in the area of the seventh cervical vertebra in the back and in the 'V' where the collar bones meet at the front of the neck. This centre manifests in the thyroid gland and controls the lower jaw, the neck, the voice, airways and lungs. It is often found to be the seat of allergies and definitely correlates with the occurrence of asthma. The metaphysical cause of asthma seems to be repressed crying or smothered love. In both these cases the person is unable to express themselves as an individual, and biting back that expression creates the problem.

The two character types within this centre are:

Underactive This person will tend to be very quiet and reserved, and probably quite timid. Usually withdrawn, this character will lack direction in their lives and tend to be very lethargic.

Overactive Here we find our objective 'doer'. This person is fairly compulsive and focuses on production in quantity rather than quality. Such people tend to be hyperactive and jittery.

The neck can be viewed as the stress barometer in a person. It is here and in the shoulders that we carry the burdens of life. When you refer to somebody being 'stiff-necked' you conjure up the picture of a rigid, tense person who seems stuck in being seen to do the right thing. It is from the throat centre that we are able to sound out the state of all other centres, and this will be dealt with more fully in the next chapter. Singing can be of great therapeutic value to both the singer by means of expression, and to the listener by associated imagery and feelings.

The spoken word has its own power, and can both hurt and inspire. Add music to the words and you have a tremendously powerful chant or ritual that works through both cerebral hemispheres and increases its effectiveness by quantum leaps. It is often in the silence after the word that the true power is felt.

Brow Chakra

In ancient belief systems the brow is said to be the centre of integrated personality. The brow expresses the qualities of will, purpose, control and ambition and is found in the centre of the forehead, just above the level of the eyebrows. This centre manifests in the pituitary gland – the master controlling gland of the endocrine system. The pituitary gland manages the activity of all other endocrine glands, and will compensate or adjust to the flow from these others. In musical terms the pituitary is the conductor of the orchestra. The brow controls the left-hemisphere functions of the brain as well as the eyes, nose, ears, sinus cavities and the nervous system. It is the centre from which you are able to be assertive.

The brow chakra polarises in two character types:

Underactive This character will have a very poor self-image with resultant low self-esteem. Such people make very poor leaders and seem to be weak-willed and have no direction in life. Very often we find they are vague and go through life as if in a dream. You may often find these people standing in the dole queue.

Overactive Here we have a very controlled and controlling type of person. This person has a strong ego, and tends to have a total disregard of others. A rigid personality type with strong mental power.

Jung made a statement that is very true for this centre. He said, 'A life without purpose is a neurotic one.' This is borne out in clinics around the world, where the hypochondriac is the person with no purpose in life.

When we talk about the brain and its various functions, do not get confused into believing that the mind is found within the brain. As leading brain surgeons will tell you, they have not yet discovered the mind! The mind is a field that exists in and around the body and works through the brain. Mental illness is very often a result of people who become polarised in the mind and lose contact with reality through the root. These people live with a picture that is not consistent with our familiar, 'consensus' reality and until we can share their picture we label them insane and lock them away. Perhaps all we need to do is to find a way of grounding their reality.

Crown Chakra

The qualities we attribute to the crown are those of consciousness, awareness, inner development and perceptions of the whole scheme of things. The crown is positioned centrally on the top of the head and manifests in the pineal gland. In Greek mythology the pineal gland was said to be the seat of the soul. The Hopi Indians in North America believed the soft spot on the top of the head was the 'open door' which received life and communication from the Creator. The consciousness principle is anchored in the crown centre, and when this is disrupted a coma will result. A coma is, of course, a loss of consciousness. The pineal gland has been the mystery gland of the system. In the past it was thought to have no function beyond the age of seven. Rudolph Steiner equated it to the emergence of permanent teeth in children. Scientists are now discovering that the pineal gland is possibly the most important of all the endocrine glands, and is beginning to take over as conductor of the orchestra. Perhaps we humans are finally entering into an age of global consciousness where personal gratification is no longer the desired goal.

Surgical exploration done between the years 1965 and 1980 has resulted in the discovery that the pineal gland is becoming larger. We can no longer refer to ourselves as being pea-brained! Autopsies show the pineal gland no longer atrophies as it has in the past, and is becoming more active with age.

The crown controls the function of the right hemisphere of the brain which has to do with non-rational perception. While the left hemisphere thinks in words the right hemisphere thinks in pictures and symbols. This centre has to do with relatedness, consciousness, intuition and transpersonal awareness.

The crown gives us two clear character types:

Underactive This person is normally limited to a physical reality and is probably very materialistic. Their energy will still be confined to the brow centre as defined previously.

Overactive The overactive crown person will tend to experience themselves as being the centre of the universe, and as such will see themselves as the saviours of humanity. They will become very distant from reality and possibly withdraw into their own dream world. It is possible for this condition to be falsely created by the misuse of hallucinogenic drugs. Here the crown centre is blasted open before it is ready to handle these energies, and cuts the individual off from any sense of reality.

Unless the energy of the crown can be integrated the person becomes so 'heavenly' that they are no earthly good. It is through the crown that we are able to access new dimensions and capacities of the mind but these need to be integrated.

With these insights into the seven major energy centres of the body we are now able to move on and begin to work with the effects of sound within the whole person.

4 SOUND AND VISUALISATION FOR HEALTH

Music has a unique effect on each individual, and can change the collective thinking of a whole nation. Cyril Scott writing in *Music* proposes that various composers have helped to change the political and moral tone of countries. He suggests that Handel by the formal character of his music was responsible for changing the morals in England from laxity to undue constraint in the early 18th century. Beethoven allowed the emotions to be set free once more, and Debussy brought in Nature music to inspire people to bring out the unseen in themselves.

Rousing music is now being used to speed up people who are very slow by nature, as well as to motivate whole groups. Classic examples of this are the military style of music which creates a sense of marching 'forever onward'. The bagpipes in Scotland were used to pipe warriors into battle, and the whole nation will still rise to the sound of *Scotland the Brave.* In more ancient cultures drums, rattles and rhythm sticks were used to pick up the tempo and slowly to increase the speed, bringing the dancers to life. Fast tempos are used in child therapy to enliven the individual, whereas hyperactive children need quiet music to relax them. It has been found that ambient music has a remarkable effect in reducing the hyperactive tempo in Down's Syndrome cases.

Relaxation techniques become vastly more effective with the use of ambient music in relaxing the mind. Research undertaken by Maxwell Cade in England using biofeedback techniques at first demonstrated the ability relaxation had in bringing the mind into an alpha rhythm pattern, but few people with the exception of certain healers and mediums could go beyond this state. He observed that as soon as non-structured ambient music was played to people in the alpha state they readily went deeper into a theta pattern. These deep states of relaxation or meditation create an infinite experience for the awareness to explore. People in these states are aware of 'thinking' from spaces outside the body. With practice we can train ourselves to enter these very relaxed states in a matter of seconds, and it is in these states that the mind becomes most productive.

It is becoming more common to hear of business meetings starting with a few moments of silent attunement. These groups report that members experience greater calm within themselves as individuals, and that less time is wasted in trying to understand the other person's point of view. It would seem that after this silent attunement the group is more likely to be functioning as a cohesive whole. The use of healing music as a focal point for silent attunement, and then as a quiet background accompaniment, could enhance the productivity of these meetings even further...

Many people have experienced the relaxing and healing effect of gently vibrating chairs or beds used in a therapeutic way. Sound is a vibration, and so music may be used as a vibrational force to reach afflicted areas. We seem to lose touch with the vibrational effect of sound. Pause for a moment and with your fingertips, block off your ears to eliminate all outside noise. Now begin to talk in a normal voice and feel how different your voice sounds. You will notice the voice seems to be vibrating from within rather than the sound being an outer manifestation. A similar experiment can be conducted simply by immersing your head under water and making audible sounds. Once again the vibrational effect will be heard to resonate through the water. Each one of us is unique in our own way, and we should never fall into the trap of comparing ourselves or our achievements with others. In Tibet, monks admitted to the monastries were each assessed for their own personal vibration and a brass bell was struck to resonate the individual's particular note. This note would be set to the vibration of that person, and it is said that no two bells were ever cast the same. A similar pattern is evident in Brazil where each person seems to develop their own rhythm. Wherever the locals congregate you may observe each person vibrating in their own particular way, giving the effect of a subtle sea of movement. Perhaps the recognition of this inner rhythm is responsible for the readiness these people have to dance, and the obvious pleasure they derive from the dance.

In Japan, atonal music has been used by the Zen Buddhist Monks for centuries in their chanting. These chants were used to confuse and disarm the rational mind, allowing the participants to experience deeper states of meditation. The effects of what we term 'New Age' music in quietening the mind have in fact been known to various cultures for many centuries. The effects of chanting in this manner are evident in most cultures of the world. In Africa, gangs of workers are able to move immense weights by encircling the object, chanting, and then applying their inner strength collectively at specific moments. In the Far East similar chants are used to prepare barefooted people to walk through pits of burning coals. This particular practice is now popular in many Western countries and is based on the belief that a focused mind has the power to do anything. In North America the American Indian used chanting to enhance a trance-like state before entering into various painful initiation rituals. One such ritual is to hang suspended by ropes attached to sharp spikes of wood inserted through the skin. It seems plausible that sound as a vibrational force was possibly used to transport the massive stone statues evident in the Easter Islands, or perhaps even used in the construction of the Pyramids.

In the Japanese map of energy patterns in the body health practitioners refer to the *Hara* centre. This centre is positioned four fingers below the navel, and corresponds with the centre of gravity of the body. It is the Hara centre that becomes the focal point for the great Sumo wrestlers. The Hara centre is, in effect, the power centre of the body, and athletes around the world have become conscious of the benefits of harnessing physical power from this point. If you observe discus throwers, for example, you will notice that they will often emit a loud yell a moment before releasing the disc. They are in effect releasing the power of the Hara, and their throw becomes similar to a volcanic eruption from this point running throughout the body to the very fingers curled around the discus. Sound, like music, is able to set the captive spirit free.

Music and sound are a vibrational energy, and can be used as such to discover and release imbalances in the human system. Stress is a state of imbalance, and the relaxing effects of ambient or healing music on these states is widely recorded. What is less commonly known is that this form of music can create the fantasy that will reveal the basic emotional blocks and decision processes in a way that is safe and less threatening than the real life situations. In his work with clients, Andrew Watson will often use a specific piece of music to create a fantasy with which the client feels safe. He will then develop the fantasy to lead the client back to early childhood days, and still within the fantasy observe what was taking place around the child. From being in a quiet, relaxed, playful state the client may experience a dramatic emotional shift as the fantasy scenario is played out. Events will then be discovered that really happened, but were erased by the conscious mind as being too painful. The client will feel the event as though it were happening in that moment, and will be able to recognise the decision the child made about itself. Having recognised this decision the child can then, with the assistance of the adult (the client), re-choose how it would like to react. In this way old behaviour patterns and belief systems may be changed.

Imagination and images, like the fantasy, are healing tools. The next time you suffer from a headache, rather than reaching for a pill, let your awareness go into the specific area of the pain. Imagine now what shape this pain takes... picture the shape clearly, and begin to see its colour and texture... become aware of the taste or smell of the shape, and then place the shape as though it were riding on the back of a wave of sound. As you release the sound see the shape fly away. This simple procedure, especially if repeated a few times, will remove the most nagging pains.

Once we have a symbolic representation of an energy we are more easily able to work with it. Dr Carl Simonton and his wife Stephanie in California, pioneered the use of visualisation and imagery in the orthodox world. Together they have dealt with terminal cancer patients, and as a complementary therapy to the orthodox treatment they began to use visualisation effectively. The Simontons asked each patient to get a clear image or symbol for their cancer. Once the patient could see the cancer clearly they then asked that an image for the active immune system be found. These two images were then brought together and developed until the immune system image was more powerful than that of the cancer. The patient was instructed to use these images creatively several times a day and to see the immune system overpowering the cancer.

In a recent case study Andrew Watson asked a patient with a massive abdominal tumour to find the image to represent the cancer. The image she discovered was that of a large black vampire, and her comment was that it was sucking her dry. The more the vampire fed off her the bigger it got, and the more wasted she became. Her immune system image was that of a shaft of white light running down her spine. In comparing the images the vampire held the balance of power. When asked to allow the immune image to develop further she reported that the light branched out to link the two kidneys, thus forming the sign of the crucifix. In mythology there are two forces the vampire cannot tolerate. These are bright white light, and the sign of the crucifix. From that moment on the immune system had power over the cancer and within months she was declared medically clear of the disease.

Some people have great difficulty in finding a suitable image, or in imagining anything there at all. These people tend to respond more favourably when exposed to music that stimulates the imagination. An Australian musician, Japetus, has developed what he calls the 'Inner Space Series'. The series consists of three tapes composed specifically for visualisation workshops presented in the book *Music for Inner Space* by Nevill Drury. Other suitable compositions include *The Ethereal Stream* by Tarshito, *The Calling* by John Richardson and *Aquamarine* by Stairway. Once again, it is the connective effect sound has between both brain hemispheres that triggers the imagery. In giving intangible energy a form to manifest in we are able to accept that it really exists, and therefore are able to work with it. In transpersonal psychology we learn to bless the obstacle. Any problems arising in our life gives us the opportunity to change. As Marilyn Ferguson writes in *The Aquarian Conspiracy*, 'Illness is potentially transformative because it can cause a sudden shift in values, an awakening'.

Creative visualisation can have a marked effect on our everyday life. For example, if you were asked to get an image of how you see yourself now, you would come up with a particular answer. Were this image not to be perfect you would automatically limit your potential. If, however, you were asked to create an image of how you would ideally like to be, and hold that image daily, the chances are you would move towards becoming that person. To quote Goethe, 'If you treat a person as they appear to be you make them less than they are. If, however, you treat a person as if they already were what they potentially could be, you make them what they should be'.

Another creative form of visualisation is to see things as if they already had happened. For example if you were selling a house, begin to visualise daily the 'sold' sign appearing outside the house, and see yourself in the agent's office exchanging contracts. Recently a friend in London presumed she had sold her home. But at the eleventh hour the sale fell through with the purchaser withdrawing. She was deeply distressed, and it was suggested she visualise the purchaser changing his mind and returning to exchange contracts. She held this visualisation over a period of three weeks, at which point the potential purchaser returned and offered her 5,000 pounds sterling more than they had agreed on in the initial instance! In all these cases the power of the image was able to rearrange circumstances. Imagine then, the results you would get from the power released when using music to accompany and transport the image.

When working with creative visualisation in this way we need to know at a deep level that it is working for us. Impatience is one of the few states that will interfere with this process. It is important to allow a *natural flow* to happen, and we can see in Nature how the best things often take time. If Nature prepares something in six months it makes a pumpkin: but to make an oak tree it takes 100 years. So if you want to be a pumpkin you can do it rapidly!

5 EXERCISES IN CREATIVE VISUALISATION

The exercises in creative visualisation presented in this chapter have been carefully prepared in a specific order, and we do suggest that initially you practise them in this order. At the beginning of each exercise we list a selection of music that we feel appropriate to enhance the experience. In the past people have found it advantageous to dictate for themselves the various steps given in the exercises, onto a tape. Be careful to allow sufficient time to elapse to carry out each step comfortably before giving the next instruction. Then as you relax and move into the exercise your tape will give you the instructions while you listen to the specific piece of music. As some of these exercises evoke very deep subconscious images we do suggest you ensure that you are undisturbed for the duration of the exercise, and allow yourself time at the end to draw and record your experience if necessary. By drawing your image or symbol at the end of a visualisation you effectively put the energy outside yourself, and can work more effectively from that perspective. An alternative way of working these exercises is to do so with a partner, where one partner will be receptive while the other partner reads the instructions while music is playing. The music we have chosen is what we have found most appropriate for most people over a period of years. There will of course, always be exceptions, and if you find a particular piece does not suit you then leave it out and let your intuition guide you towards the correct music. Lists provided at the end of this book may help you in your selection.

The Body

Ken Dychtwald has written a wonderful book called *Bodymind* in which he correlates the effect emotional and psychological activity and experience have on the body. He demonstrates clearly how a body can often be a perfect reflection of our own life's history, present state of being, and potential for continued growth and development. He deals effectively with each area of the body in turn, and brings our attention to the effects early toilet training, for example, have on our emotional expression and freedom to enjoy pleasure. The neck he maps as the stress barometer and he deals at length with the amount of tension and past patterning we carry in our shoulders. Begin to look at your friends or associates and observe how they carry their shoulders. People with rounded shoulders tend to be overburdened, while those with very raised shoulders seem fearful.

Square shoulders indicate power and self assurance. Shoulders pulled forward show a certain vulnerability while those pulled back suggest a lack of expression. A person with very narrow shoulders will tend to be very dependent.

The body holds a tremendous amount of information in relation to the male/female balance within the individual. In general terms the left-hand side of the body reflects the feminine while the right-hand side reflects the masculine. By observing the differences in body structure between the two sides we are able to assess certain strengths or weaknesses relevant to a given person.

Each person has a particular part of the body where stress is first noticed, and this varies greatly between people. It has been suggested that people who suffer hair-loss carry their tension in their scalp. Those who tend to suffer from stomach ulcers obviously deposit their tension in that area. The importance in working with the body is to pay attention to the areas where you carry the most stress. By paying attention to the stress in a relaxed state you are able to transform it. Refusal to acknowledge stress gives it power over us, and not only does it not go away but in fact it goes deeper into the body.

The first step in any visualisation exercise is to become physically relaxed. To this end most forms of healing music will suffice, but we would specifically suggest the following titles: *Cirrus* by John Richardson, *Emergence* by Med Goodall, *The Twilight of Dreams* by Alan Hinde, *Breath on the Water* by Tarshito or *Peace, Tranquility*, or *Harmony* by David Sun. For this exercise we suggest you lie down comfortably, perhaps with a small cushion under your head and ensure that all clothing is loose.

Exercise 1

Begin now with a few deep breaths to let go of the day and let your awareness flow down to your toes. Clench your toes as tightly as you can bending them downwards... then flex them as high as you can... then bend them double once again feeling the pressure this creates in the arch of the foot. Now relax your toes completely... let them go. Bring your awareness gently up to your ankles... tense your ankles making them as tight as you can... and then rotate the ankle joints as far round in a circular motion as you can get them to move... now relax your ankles. Become aware of your calves, and clench your calves as tightly as you can. Hold that tension... and now relax them. Move your awareness up to your knees... tense your knees tightly pulling in the kneecap... after a while let them go, and bring your awareness up to your thighs. Once again tense every muscle in your thigh... tighter still... and then relax them completely. Allow your awareness to move up to your buttocks and genitals and clench the muscles in these areas as tightly as you can... hold the tension for a while... then relax. Focus now on your lower abdomen and contract the muscles there as tightly as you can... and relax bringing your awareness up to your chest. Allow your breath to expand your chest as far as it will go... hold it there for a moment before whooshing all the air out of your lungs until your chest is totally contracted. Repeat this three times. Become aware now of your fingers and hands... clench your fingers as tightly as possible before letting them go, and do the same for your forearms, elbows and upper arms. As you begin to focus on your shoulders pull your shoulders up towards your ears as far as they will go... then let them down again... now draw your shoulders forward as far as they will go... hold them there for a moment... then relax them... and now back as far as they will go, pushing against the floor... and relax. Moving now to your neck... tense the whole of your neck as tight as you can before relaxing... now gently let your head roll first to the left and then to the right as far as it will comfortably go, returning to a central position and relax. Bringing your awareness now to your head, begin by screwing up your face as tightly as you can. Feel the muscles in your forehead, eyes, nose, mouth and cheeks pulling tightly together... and relax. Then open your mouth as wide as possible, sticking your tongue far out and at the same time opening your eyes as wide as possible... feel every muscle stretching... and relax once more. As you do so let go of your mind and become aware of a total stillness within as you lie relaxed and let the music flow through you. You are aware only of your gentle breathing and the feel of the sound moving gently through your body. If possible, remain in this relaxed state until the music has finished.

Nature

The Hopi Indians of North America thought the human body and the body of the earth were made in the same way (see Frank Waters: *The Book of the Hopi*). In the so-called civilised countries we tend to lose sight of the fact that humans are an integral part of Nature. For some reason we believe we have the power to control Nature, and that is our biggest mistake. As Rolling Thunder states, 'The nature of man is identical with the nature of the universe. Thus to learn about his nature he needs to study Nature itself.' Chief Seattle in his famous reply to the President of America, when asked to sell his land to the white man, spoke about the oneness of all life and he claimed that 'to harm the earth is to harm ourselves. All life is one.' You only have to stop and begin to work with Nature to see the truth of this statement. Recently residents on a property outside London were threatened by the local council with chemical insecticides and weedkillers to control snails breeding in their wild garden. The people concerned refused to have any chemicals used on the property, and were given a two-week period of grace in which to control the snail population. Having made this strong statement of their alignment with Nature, Nature took over. The very next day a new species of bird was observed to be feeding in the garden, and this was the song thrush. The primary diet of the song thrush is snails. When the inspectors returned after the two-week period was up they could find no evidence of snails on the property.

Not only will Nature begin to work with you it will also begin to protect you. This was made evident when Andrew Watson spent some time alone on a deserted island. He discovered very quickly that the island had no fear, and as a result he was unable to kill any living thing while he was there. He chose to work with the forces of Nature. On several occasions he attempted to swim out to a reef some 300 feet away from the island, but on each occasion was met by a large shark swimming directly towards him, which promptly ended his adventure. After this happening every day over a period of weeks, he determined to challenge the shark and reach the outer reef. That next morning Nature had picked up his intent, and there were five sharks waiting for him. It was only when the yacht returned to collect him that he discovered there was a dangerous current running through the channel between his island and the reef that would have taken him straight out to sea. He then understood why Nature had chosen to intervene.

One of the most important healing places available to us is our very own quiet Nature spot, and we will now set out to discover this for ourselves.

The music we suggest for the next exercise could be the playing of Nature's sounds such as *Island Called Paradise*, *Secret Garden* or *Restful Sounds* all by David Sun, or musical compositions such as *The Fairy Ring* and *Silver Wings* by Mike Rowland, *Reverence* by Terry Oldfield, or *Fragile Shoreline* by Mike Brooks.

Exercise 2

Sit or lie comfortably and let your body relax. As you relax begin to picture yourself standing in your very own quiet place in Nature. This place may be real or imaginary. It is here that you feel totally relaxed, protected and nourished. Begin to look around and take in every detail of this, your very own, quiet place. Allow this place to become real for you. Feel the temperature... become aware of the fragrance in the air... see the way the light plays through the foliage... begin to hear the sounds in this your very own quiet place (allow several minutes to pass while you fully inhabit this quiet place). Become aware that this place is available to you at any moment during the day or night. You only have to wish to be there for it to happen. In this quiet place you are able to relax and find peace, harmony and healing. Gently take a few deep breaths and feel the essence of this very special place. Touch every cell in the body. Very gently, when you feel quite ready, take one last look around this, your very own quiet place and quietly let your awareness return to wherever you happen to be. Perhaps you can allow a symbol to come to you that will represent this special place and use the symbol to return there in the future.

The Breath

We often refer to the breath of life, but how much time do we spend focusing on how we breathe? Very often the old conditioning of 'belly in, chest out' still applies. This effectively freezes the diaphragm and allows us to use only the upper portion of our lungs. This breathing pattern has brought world recognition to one Harley Street heart specialist. He discovered that most of the patients referred to him with high blood pressure or slight heart defects had in fact nothing wrong with them on a physical level. Their problems lay in their form of hyperventilation, where they were breathing with only the upper portion of the lungs. The breaths were necessarily fairly shallow and rapid, causing the blood stream to absorb too high a percentage of oxygen. He employed a masseuse to teach these patients how to breathe into the belly, thereby freeing the diaphragm. To do this effectively the patient had to lie on their back with one hand placed on their lower abdomen and the other hand on their chest. They were then instructed to breathe in without any movement at all in the chest area. The only way they could achieve this was by extending the abdomen, thus pulling down the diaphragm and sucking the air in. With practice these patients were able to perfect this pattern of breathing, and they no longer exhibited the original symptoms.

This form of connected breath has long been part of Yogic tradition. Practitioners of Yoga divide the lung into three sections: upper, middle and lower, and each section has three components, front, middle and back. So, in effect, they divide the lung into 18 separate compartments and learn through exercises to breathe into each one individually. For our purposes we will do a three-stage breathing exercise. From a position of full exhalation, begin by extending the abdomen to draw the diaphragm down and suck air into the lower portion of the lung only. Once the lower segment of the lung is filled begin to expand the chest filling the mid lung, and once you feel no more air can be drawn into the lungs the third stage is reached by a slight upward and outward movement of the shoulders which effectively opens the upper lung segments. As you exhale you repeat the sequence breathing out from the belly first, then the chest and finally the shoulders. We suggest fairly lively music for this exercise as found in *The Calling* by John Richardson or *Glass Isle* by Michael Law.

Exercise 3

Relax your body and imagine you are standing at the edge of a deep well. See yourself bending down and collecting ten smooth pebbles which you find on the ground. With the chest fully extended drop one pebble down into the well, and as the pebble falls you begin to breathe out in the correct sequence, having fully exhaled all breath as the pebble strikes the bottom of the well. As your awareness returns up to the surface you begin to breathe in, starting by extending the abdomen. By the time you are ready to drop the next pebble your lungs are fully extended and you repeat the cycle following the pebble down as you breathe out. Do this gently with all ten pebbles. Three lots of ten pebbles form a round, and we suggest you do at least three full rounds. On completion of your rounds, lie quietly and feel how energised your body is as you relax to the music.

General Health

Any form of disease, or dis-ease, reflects a state of imbalance in the system. In some way through our lifestyle or our belief systems we have helped to create this state of imbalance. If we had the power to upset the system in this way, we also have the power to correct it. Too often in the past we have viewed ourselves as the victim of disease. We believed in some way that we were walking along minding our own business when a virus leapt out of the bushes and attacked us! The past pattern, when this occurred, was to take our body to the mechanic and ask that it be fixed. Thankfully, most people are no longer happy with handing over total responsibility for their bodies.

Within each and every one of us there lies an intelligence that is constantly renewing and revitalising every cell in our body. There is no need for us to have any conscious control over this intelligence. In effect it operates despite our efforts. All we have to do is align ourselves with it in order for healing to take place. As Marilyn Ferguson states in *The Aquarian Conspiracy*, 'The healer inside us is the wisest, most complex, integrated entity in the Universe.' 'She carries on to state, 'It is as if there is a life force or ordering principle ready to re-establish our natural state of wholeness and health if we can just drop the barriers of negative expectations. Healing comes as a direct result of perceiving ourselves as whole', and this happens 'when we re-establish our sense of balanced relationship with the universe through a change of mind; a transformation in attitudes, values and beliefs.'

The music we suggest for the following visualisation is *Solstice* by John Richardson, *Serenity* by David Sun and *Music for Healing* by Arden Wilken.

Exercise 4

Begin to visualise yourself standing in a field of flowers. Feel the sun warming your head and shoulders, and become aware of a gentle breeze fanning your cheek as you look around the field. Spend a few moments becoming aware of yourself standing in the field. Now gently begin to breathe using the previous sequence. As you breathe in imagine the air you breathe is filled with sparkling white light, and feel this white light being drawn into your body. On the out breath begin to see the cloudiness as the breath from the body meets the outside air. It is almost as though the outgoing breath carries any negativity with it. Spend a few moments breathing in this way until the out breath becomes clear as all impurities leave the body.

See yourself now turning around in the centre of this field and there in front of you you discover a large clear bubble. Feel yourself moving into the centre of this bubble and stand there comfortably as the bubble begins to rise up into the air. You seem to be suspended in the centre of the bubble and the bubble itself seems suspended in space. You float freely, higher and higher, and as you do so you begin to feel your whole body being revitalised. Every cell in your body is in perfect health. Spend a little while experiencing this state. Gently your bubble begins to drift back to earth, to land softly in the centre of your field, and as you emerge from the bubble you notice that you are now exactly as you would ideally like to be. It is as if the old you went up in the bubble and has been transformed into a totally new, revitalised, healthy being. Feel the vibration of this new healthy person flow through every cell in your body as you lie quietly, and allow the music to carry you along.

The Root

The root has to do with our survival on this earth plane and in order to survive we need to align ourselves with the Earth Mother. In all the older tribal customs around the world the people respected the earth as their mother, and their dances reflected their need to reconnect with the earth. These tribal dances invariably contain sequences of stamping the earth in a rhythmic way. The wise people in these tribes knew that this was how to feed the mother.

As acupuncture can liberate energies trapped in the body, so the stamping of feet frees the energy of the earth. The most powerful native forms always contained musical rhythm, vigorous dance and group chanting. The instruments used in the ancient tribal rituals were usually symbolic of the earth itself, and throughout the world today you still find instruments like the drums from Africa and the didgeridoo from Australia. These instruments are timeless and were evolved to evoke the Nature spirits. Instruments very similar to these are found in most countries around the world from Tibet to the Amazon.

The root is the first of three centres that compose the lower half of the bodymind, and all three are concerned with the private, self-supportive and the self-grounding aspects of our being. All three centres are enhanced by very strong dance forms, all of which have to do with survival.

Music focused on the seven major chakras has a twofold effect. One form of sound or music can be used to excite a strong reaction from the centre, while the second more general type can be used to feed and balance.

Types of music to excite the root would be heavy African drumming (as in Burundi), some basic didgeridoo sounds and tribal chants. During the following visualisation we would suggest you played either *Meetings With Remarkable Alloys* by Chris Campbell or a more gentle piece, *Spirit of the Red Man*, by John Richardson.

Exercise 5

Sit or lie quietly and relax your body. Free your mind and gently allow yourself to flow backwards in time... let the years roll away... right the way back to when you were young... to being a child... back to being a baby. Let time continue backwards through the moment of birth and back into the womb, right back to the moment of conception. At this point time begins to move forward once more and you begin to visualise how you survived your time in the womb... how you survived the birth process... and how you survived the first few weeks of your life. Recall, perhaps, an initial desire to live – and a search for the breast. And as time moves forward begin to recall a time of feeling great love... and a time of feeling rejection... and begin to see how you survived the first few months of your life. As time moves forward begin to see all your patterns of survival as you return back to this present day. Allow an image or a symbol to form that would represent the quality of your survival energy. See this image or symbol as fully as you can, and when you feel it appropriate gently draw your image or symbol in colour.

The Sacral

The sacral is a very personal centre and is often experienced by using all the senses. It is said to be the centre of freedom. As we descovered earlier one of the qualities of this centre is sensuality. To what extent do you allow yourself to use your senses fully each day? Dance forms applicable to this centre are both strong and sensual at the same time. Let your fancies flow freely for a moment and consider what form of dance or movement you would use within this centre. Being of such a personal nature it is difficult to define a form of music that would suit most people. We would suggest you try *Images* or *The Experience* both by David Satchell, or perhaps *The Ultimate Melody* by Baldursson, Hurdle and Ricotti.

Exercise 6

Relax once again and free both body and mind. Once again allow time to go backwards, back to being a tiny baby and begin to recall the wonder of your first sense of touch... perhaps touching your mother's body... or of being touched... or of touching yourself. Recall an early sense of taste and being fulfilled. Begin to recall how all your senses served you when you were very tiny and as you begin to grow up begin to get a sense of an early form of creativity and how you reacted to being touched. Recall a time of exploring your whole body and a sense of discovering the difference between boys and girls. As time moves forward begin to recall the changes you may have felt around puberty... or the feel of attraction for some other person. Begin to recall how your body responded to love and how much in fact you were able to love your own body. Become aware of yourself as a sensual being, and see how much personal expression you have in your life. Once again as you float on the music allow an image or a symbol to form that could represent the state of your sacral centre and when you are ready record your image or symbol on paper and relax once more to the music.

The Solar Plexus

We have discussed the effect Beethoven's music had on people's emotions in Europe, and by now we are well aware of the effect rhythm and harmony have on our feeling states. Can you remember a time, walking alone along a dark road at night when you began to whistle, hum or even sing to lift your spirits? You were in fact using the vibration of sound to strengthen your inner resolve. In a similar way, military marches feed energy into the system and create a sense of excitement. Funeral dirges, on the other hand produce a feeling of sadness or depression. Many cultures use singing and chanting as a means of expressing grief, and will very often break into dance and song as a means of transmuting the energy. A more recent form of working with the energy of sound is through the use of Toning. In this practice you allow the sound of the pain, be it physical or emotional, to be expressed and you continue to sound it out vocally as loudly as you feel is appropriate. As you continue to allow the sound to flow you will begin to notice the energy within the sound is changing and the tone of the sound may well be lightening.

Eventually a deep sad moan might be transformed into a clear crystal note without any effort from the practitioner. At this point the energy of the experience will have changed and freed itself from the body.

The body is literal and cannot tell the difference between real threat and perceived threat. A particular worry or negative expectation will translate into a physical illness because the body feels as if it were in danger. From this you can see that if you imagine yourself to be a failure you will undoubtedly fail. If you think you're going to be afraid you will surely feel fear. If you believe yourself to be fat and ugly your body will resonate to these states too. It is therefore vital that we learn to express real and imagined feelings as they occur. Here again, tribal groups have the advantage because for them dancing is a natural way of expressing whatever happens in the course of each day.

Music to evoke a response in this centre could be taken from the *Music from the World of Islam: flutes and trumpets*, or once again various African or Balinese chants. To work with and support the solar plexus we could recommend *Aquamarine* by Stairway, *Sunrise* by David Sun or *The Enchanter* by Tim Wheater.

Exercise 7

This exercise can be done in any position but we suggest you begin by standing freely. Become aware of the solar plexus as the feeling centre and begin to allow a feeling of sadness to come over you. As you do so, allow your body to take on the posture of sadness. Feel how your body responds to this feeling state, and pause here for a while. Allow that sadness now to turn to anger, and once again feel how your body reacts to the feeling of anger and allow your body to take on a stance or position that would support this feeling. Continue in your own time working in the same way with the following feeling states:

– fear – bravery – loneliness – impatience – frustration –
– resentment – calmness – happiness – feeling loved –

Let go of all these feeling states and allow an image or a symbol that would represent the quality of the energy involved. Once again, in your own time, draw your image or symbol, and then relax as the music flows through you.

The Heart

This centre, as we discovered earlier, controls the immune system and is therefore of vital importance in the healing process. When you really care about somebody you talk about them 'touching your heart'. Being a more transpersonal form of energy this centre is more concerned with global issues rather than personal gratifications. Some forms of Baroque music were set to 60 beats per minute, and had a marked calming effect on the courtiers exposed to it over the centuries. A great number of ambient or healing music titles are set in the same rhythm. This type of music effectively paces the heartbeat to achieve mental efficiency and alertness. It would seem that clearing the space within allows so much more input to be handled by the mind. The heart serves to guard against hurt and attack but, in doing so, limits warmth and nourishment. Thus when we refer to somebody as being hard-hearted, we also imply that they cannot receive warmth for themselves. The inner state affects the outer reality. The heart in healing terms, is the transformer used to convert universal energy into the healing force of unconditional love. This is a love that has no expectations and no demands, and is given freely with no thought of any return.

Music used to trigger this centre could well include the natural sounds of whales and dolphins. Pachelbel's *Canon* is a classical piece that invariably produces a similar effect. The music we would recommend using for the following visualisation could be selected from *Great Peace* by Robert Martin, *Quiet Water* by Fitzgerald and Flanagan, *The Response* by John Richardson, *Edge of Dreams* by Phil Thornton, or *Deep Enchantment* by David Sun.

Exercise 8

Sit or lie comfortably and relax your body and mind. Begin now to imagine the closed bud of a flower you know will have twelve golden petals and a radiant blue centre.

As you visualise this closed bud the sun rises over the horizon and shines down to warm and enliven this plant. The closed bud begins to stir with the new life-force, and very slowly the outer petals begin to open. Visualise the sun continuing to shine down on this opening bud as the petals gently draw back one by one, eventually revealing a glimpse of this radiant blue centre. As the sun strikes the blue in the centre of this opening bud the centre is energised and begins to spin on itself. As the twelve golden petals open fully outwards the radiant blue centre begins to spin more and more swiftly, and starts to expand over the golden petals. Visualise the sun energising this now open flower as the blue centre gets bigger and bigger, encompassing the whole flower, and then begins to fill the space around it... Further and further the spinning radiant blue centre expands, covering everything in its path until it extends all the way to the horizon and beyond. As this radiant blue colour flows out over the earth it comes to troubled spots around the world – places that are in conflict, drought and starvation. This radiant blue energy feels the pain and suffering of these various peoples, and feels too the pain of the ravaged earth. As the sun continues to enliven the golden petalled flower this radiant blue energy is able to flow around the whole planet bringing with it peace, harmony and healing. As the world is healed, feel within yourself great joy in your heart.

Gently become centred once again in yourself, and allow an image or a symbol to form that would represent the quality of energy found within the heart. In your own time draw or record your experience. Once again relax as the healing music flows through you.

The Throat

Creativity, productivity and expression are the qualities concerned here. 'In the beginning was the Word...' forms one of the primal statements in the Bible, and suggests that the vibrational energy of sound is the creative force behind all matter. Pythagoras noted this in a slightly different way when he said, 'All things are constructed on harmonic patterns.' The strict laws that govern all creation leave no space for chance happening or coincidence. Coincidence is nothing more than God's way of remaining anonymous.

Music in industry is being used on a large scale at present to increase productivity. It stands to reason that the more relaxed and aware members of the workforce are, the more they will achieve. A side-effect of creating a happier atmosphere in the work-force has been a substantial decrease in the absenteeism rate. The standard of workmanship has also been vastly improved.

Spontaneous expression is a facet of life that is sadly on the decrease in the Western world. We seem to have lost our natural ability for dance and music, and are no longer willing participants in these art forms. You only have to watch a carnival in Trinidad or the Ketjak Monkey Dance in Bali to realise how far removed we are from our own natural ability to move and sound out the joys of being alive. Regrettably the effects of a staid Victorian era still seem to have a strong effect on us.

The human voice is one of the finest musical instruments we have. Not only does it have a fairly large range, but it is also able to convey every form of feeling by its tonal expression. One word can be given many different meanings by the tone in which it is delivered. Think for a moment of the different tones in a parent's voice when reprimanding a child, or looking at a new-born baby, or gazing into the eyes of a loved one. The sound of a boys' choir evokes angelic images, while a barber shop quartet carries us along on its harmony. Without understanding the language at all we are able to know the meaning in many tribal chants and deeper rituals. The tenor of the chant presents us with a whole picture at a feeling level. We discovered earlier how chanting is used to increase physical prowess. Certain chants have been developed to combat pain in a similar way, removing the participants from normal awareness and creating altered states of consciousness where pain no longer registers. Over the centuries man has found different ways to amplify and extend the effect of the human voice and wind instruments also do this effectively, as we all know. If we trace the evolution of the wind instruments towards their origin we might discover the trail leads us through natural forms like the didgeridoo, back to the blowing stones found in areas in Africa, the Easter Islands and pre-historic Britain. These blowing stones were used in earth rituals, and seemed to perform the role of extending human expression to reach through to the womb of Mother Earth.

In the Easter Islands fishermen use the voice and image together in rituals designed to attract particular species of fish before they set out on fishing expeditions. The Elders in these rituals use strings in a similar way to the method we used as children when we made cat's cradles with string intertwined through our fingers. They have particular patterns to represent each species of fish, and a chant to match. Once they have created the image, and therefore the thought form, together with the vibration through the chant, they then set out in their boats and find their catch is limited to the species they had wanted...

The throat can be used as a centre of expression for all the lower energy centres, and allows us to get in touch with the feeling states in each centre through the use of sound. In workshop situations, people are asked to allow a sound for each of the lower centres to emerge in sequence and be sounded out. This exercise has a dynamic effect on clearing out any residual trauma that may be locked in these lower centres.

For our use in the following exercise we suggest lively, expressive music such as *Circle of Dreams* by Leonard Ellis or perhaps *Devotion* by John Richardson.

Exercise 9

Begin to relax once more, free your mind, and allow time to move backwards. Begin to go back to a time when you were young, and even further to a time when you were a child. As a child, begin gently to recall how you expressed yourself...

Recall the first time you achieved something on your own... and sense the pride you felt with that achievement... Recall how spontaneous you were as a child. As time moves forward, begin to see how that spontaneity was perhaps influenced by people around you... Recall the first time you had to stand up and speak in public... and how that felt for you. As time goes forward get a sense of how you express yourself now... and become aware of the times at which you do not express yourself clearly. What is it that limits your free spontaneous expression?... What do you need within yourself in order to become more expressive? Begin now to get a sense of the form of creativity that would be best suited to you. After a while, allow an image or a symbol to form that represents your creative and expressive energy. Record that image or symbol as best you can and then lie and relax as you are carried along by the music.

The Brow

Music tends to stimulate our natural curiosity. Through the effect of music we are able to cultivate right-brain functions and thereby use images and colours to weave webs of fantasy that often lead us into areas of the higher unconscious – the breeding ground of new ideas and creative forms. It is therefore natural to assume that the absence of art and music can have a retarding effect on the development of the brain, and especially on linking the two hemispheres together. It has been found that ambient music can lead to greater achievement in both mathematics and the sciences, and helps the mind to become alert and inquisitive. The focus in the mind centre is on will and purpose, and will can be used in both positive and negative ways. Music was a strong component of traditional witch-doctors' rituals in sending curses to people over a distance. Through movement, dance and chanting, the witch-doctor would use specific wilful instructions to impart the spell and then send the spell, riding as it were on the back of the created sound, to the often unsuspecting victim. The power of such a curse is undeniable, and modern science is often unable to determine the cause of death of the victim. This clearly illustrates the polarity you will find in every life-force. Energy may be wilfully used either constructively or destructively. Enrico Caruso, the singer, could break a glass with his voice, demonstrating one of the negative applications!

Ambient music, or healing music, that allows us to enter the meditative state induces the production of neuro-peptides and these play a significant part in reducing the perception of pain. We will deal with this more fully in a later exercise dealing with pain.

Music suitable for evoking the response in this centre could be *Ascension* by Clifford White, *Visions of Paradise* by Japetus, or *Awakenings* by Tim Wheater.

Exercise 10

Once again relax and let time take you back to being a child. As this young person begin to recall a time when you overcame a fear and you did something... and recall a time when you acted against the advice of your elders... or a time when you stuck to your convictions. Recall now a time of experiencing great control in your life... and another time when you lost control... and another time when you willed something to happen. When you are ready, begin to recall a time when you had great purpose in your life, and how that felt for you, and finally recall a time when you chose to change. Allow an image or symbol to come that represents the quality of the energy involved in all these times, and take a moment to draw your energy symbol while you listen to the music.

The Crown

As you now know, the Crown stimulates the function of the right hemisphere of the brain. It is through this hemisphere that we are able to access new dimensions and capacities of the mind. It is here that we create the images for change, and the imagination becomes our most powerful healing tool. Music activates the flow of stored memory material across the *corpus callosum* uniting both sides of the brain and thereby infinitely increasing our potential. It is noise, the unacceptable form of levels of sound, that stops this mind connection and creative process.

Melanin, a secretion of the pineal gland, activates the neuro-transmitters capable of converting light energy into sound energy and back again. The pituitary gland itself is light-sensitive in a subjective sense and the more we are able to attune to the function of the Crown the more we are able to 'see'. It is here that the Eastern concept of the 'third eye' manifests for us.

Various cultures, as we have mentioned previously, use sound to activate responses in a person. The Crown, in a sense, links us to the heavens, so what better form of stimulation for this centre than the angelic boys' choirs of Vienna or Westminster? The sound produced by the pan-pipes has a magical, ethereal quality, and you have only to listen to a master like Zamfir to be transported to magical heights. It is interesting to note that pan-pipes are native to cultures as diverse as those of Eastern Europe, South America and the Solomon Islands. In ancient Greece Aeolian harps would be positioned on certain hilltops to be plucked by the wind, and the music they made was considered to be the natural voice of the Gods.

When a child is born, the Crown centre is very open and the child has access to all knowledge. Regrettably most children are slowly conditioned to mistrust their own inner knowing. It would seem, in a sense, that our purpose in life is aimed at recreating this open, all-inclusive state of mind.

Musical pieces we would recommend here include 'Gregorian Chants' sung by the Benedictine Nuns, 'Freefall' by Malcolm Harrison, 'Cascade' by Terry Oldfield, or perhaps 'Inner Harmony' by Arden Wilken.

Exercise 11

Begin to go back in time once more and experience yourself as a young baby who resonates with the wisdom of the ages through an open Crown centre. Begin to get a sense of the child's perception of the connectedness of all things, that deep sense of Oneness. It is as though you had great inner wisdom and knowing. As time moves forward, begin to recall the stage at which you started to doubt, and began to 'close down'. Get in touch with the feelings the child must have experienced when blocking-off access to the deeper wisdom. Stay with this feeling for a while, and then gently allow yourself to move forward to a time when you began to sense some inner growth once more. Begin to observe how this emerging sense perhaps began to change your life. Acknowledge in yourself a time when you had what you might call a 'peak' experience. This could be an overpowering sense of Oneness while walking under the stars at night, or watching a beautiful sunset, or a time when your mind seemed to move into a new dimension. As you review these times be aware of the effect they may have had on your life. Perhaps they signalled a point of change in your attitudes or approach to life? Begin now to imagine how you could possibly link into these states of awareness once more, for it is in these altered states of consciousness that you are able to link with your higher self. Begin now to allow an image or a symbol to come to you that could represent the energy involved in these altered states, and spend a moment drawing and recording your experience. Then lie back and allow yourself to float free.

The Whole

In life all things are connected – nothing exists in isolation. In a natural state everything that exists is in the correct and balanced relationship with every other thing. There is no chance happening, and all forms relate together in what we might term the dance of life. There is a constant interplay, and this interplay is reflected both within and without. Within ourselves each chakra or energy centre has a relationship with each other centre. This holds true at a cellular level for every cell of any particular organ works with the similar cells within that organ to create the whole. The organs themselves work together, one with the other, in building the person and in the same way people are meant to work together to build a collective consciousness.

In ancient China the healers had what we now know was a geomancy compass. On this compass was plotted the planets and the heavens and every characteristic of the earth was marked clearly in its specific relation with every other one. When man then wanted to build a house or plough a field or alter the landscape in some way the healer was called and the geomancy compass first checked so that everything remained in the right relationship with everything else. If only the whole world had been built that way! We have tended to lose touch with our connectedness with the whole of mankind. We have divided the earth into various countries with boundaries and border control posts. We have separated the people of the earth into their various tribes and we try to keep them all apart. We have indeed lost sight of the sense of the oneness of all life, the oneness of all people, the oneness of the planet.

So it is with the chakras and with the energy fields of the body. Every centre has an effect on every other centre. All our centres – all 1000 of them – are connected in a correct pattern. It is the correctness of this pattern that allows us to be in optimal health once the dynamic flow of energy through the whole system is disrupted with inexperience – the disease of being off balance. With the major seven energy centres there are three linkages that are important. The first is between the *Brow* and the *Root*, the second between the *Throat* and the *Sacral*, and the third between the *Heart* and *Solar Plexus*. These three pairs of centres seem to complement each other very strongly and where one shows a lack of harmony or fulfilment the other will tend to compensate for it.

We suggest at this point that you spread out the seven drawings you have made over the seven last exercises. Spread them out in order starting closest to you with the drawing you made for the Root, then the Sacral and so on up to the Crown furthest away from you. You have created here a very simplistic map of the psyche, and an experienced person will be able to read your map as though they were reading your life.

Spend a moment now, looking at your series of drawings. Begin to notice which particular drawings look very strong or powerful, and which ones seem to be rather weak. What particular patterns begin to emerge as you look at your seven drawings. The stronger the drawing, or the more colour used, the stronger that centre, or the more attention you are paying to that area of your life at this moment. If, for example, you have a Solar Plexus drawing that lacks substance, it could be that you are not in touch with the emotional side of your nature. Now look for the connectedness through all your seven drawings. Is there a sense of flow? If not, at what points does the flow seem to break? These are the areas that you need to concentrate on in your own life.

The following exercise can be used to unite these centres together. Working from the Root through to the Crown and then beyond you bring the energy of the earth up through the *Sushumna*, or Central Nervous Column to unite with the energy of heaven. You are, in effect, linking Mother Earth with Father Heaven. This exercise is best done sitting erect so that your Root centres link with the earth and the Crown points towards the heavens.

Exercise 12

Spend a few moments relaxing your body whilst sitting erect and become aware of your breathing. Feel the breath moving right the way down into your belly and, as it does so, feel the muscles of the pelvis relax. Bring your whole awareness now down into the Root situated around the coccyx at the top end of the pubic bone. Become aware of this Root chakra and the qualities of power of survival and aggression linking us to the earth plane. Let the energy from your breathing fill and activate this centre and dwell here for a moment feeling the state of function of your Root chakra. (Allow a few moments for yourself to experience the energy of this centre.)

Begin now to visualise your awareness moving up from the Root to the Sacral centre and feel that about an inch or three centimetres below the navel. The Sacral centre has the qualities of sensuality, sexuality and personal creativity. Spend a while feeling this centre in your own body (pause), then allow your awareness to move up to the Solar Plexus. Feel the soft spot in your tummy just near the sternum where the ribs divide. The Solar Plexus is the emotional centre. Allow your awareness to fill this centre and feel the state of function of this centre in yourself. (Pause).

Now let your awareness move up to the Heart and feel the heart functioning centrally in your chest. The Heart is the centre of unconditional love. The love of the whole, the love that has no boundaries, no expectations, and no demands. The love of the Heart centre encompasses all life. It feels for humanity. It experiences the joy and the pain of Nature. Spend a while experiencing this centre in yourself. (Pause).

Tend now to allow the energy to move up to the Throat, the centre of creativity, production and expression. As you become aware of this centre, become aware also of any tension or tightness within your throat. As your awareness dwells within the Throat centre begin to be aware of what other centres can express themselves through the throat, and which centres are withheld from having that expression.

Let your awareness now gently rise to the position of the Brow, located centrally on the forehead. This is the centre of will, purpose, ambition, control. As your awareness dwells within the centre begin to contemplate the purpose of your life. (Pause).

And now let your awareness float up to the top of your head where you will find the energy of the Crown. The Crown connects us to the flow of life. The consciousness principle is anchored within this centre. From within the Crown we are able to see the whole pattern in life, and not just get caught up in the everyday occurrences or seeming problems.

Uniting from this centre you have the overview of your own life. While within the centre you are able to direct your life purpose. How would you like to see your life unfolding? Allow your awareness now to rise up above the top of your head, floating freely above you, moving higher and higher... and able to more through whatever obstacle might be above your head... higher and higher into the atmosphere. As you rise up above the earth plane you become formless. There are no boundaries. Everything becomes one. You begin to experience yourself as being the *whole universe.*

Spend a little while experiencing this state of total oneness and freedom. Very gently now you begin to be aware of a sense of movement downwards once more. It is as though as you begin the journey downwards you begin once again to take form slowly, gently. This form now begins to move back, back through the universe, back to being centred above the top of your head, and then very gently into the Crown centre. Become aware as the energy that is you moves through the Crown, through the Brow, the Throat, the Heart, the Solar Plexus, the Sacral, down through the Root into the earth itself. Like a tree, you connect heaven and earth, connect father and mother, connect levity and gravity. Very gently allow your awareness to re-centre in the area of the Heart, and become fully conscious once more.

This meditation is well suited to the music of Ojas, *The Seven Levels* of Man or to Japetus' *Kundalini Yoga* tape which is part of his Inner Space series.

The Transpersonal

It has been our custom as enquiring human beings to search for a teacher. In the past we've always searched for a teacher *somewhere out there.* We need somebody older and wiser than ourselves to guide us through life. As a child we looked to our parents. At school we looked to our teachers. Once we left school we looked for whoever we could find to give us guidance and help.

Many people have turned to the gurus of the East or the so-called 'enlightened Masters'. There is a very strong belief system in the East that you cannot approach God except through the medium of a guru. In principle we agree with this statement. But the point that people don't seem to realise is that our own 'transpersonal' self can act as that guru. We no longer have to search for the teacher out there somewhere in the world. Nowadays more and more people are turning within to make contact with their own higher selves. The higher self or transpersonal self acts as our intermediary to God. By tuning in to our own inner teacher we are able to find the answer to any question that might be bothering us.

There are many ways of contacting the teacher within ourselves. For our purposes here, we will refer to this teacher as a 'wise person'. Allow this wise person to take on whatever form is appropriate for you. These visualisations are often best done in silence, but if you like background music we would suggest *The Twilight of Dreams* by Alan Hinde.

Exercise 13

Sit comfortably and begin to relax your body and free your mind. As you relax, begin to conjure up the picture of your very own quiet place in Nature. Allow this place to become real for you and begin to inhabit it fully. Remind yourself of everything that exists in this quiet place. You will recall that being here gives you access to peace, to harmony, to nourishment and to healing. Spend a moment being in your very own quiet place. (Pause). As you occupy this, your very own quiet place, imagine now you look up and there in the distance you see the figure of a person approaching. As the figure approaches where you are, you become aware that it is the figure of a very wise person. You allow this person to come closer and you invite this wise person to come and share your own Nature spot. The wise person has come to tell you something, and you relax and listen to what the wise person has to say. You are able to ask questions of the wise person, and you listen eagerly to the wise person's reply. (Allow time for a full dialogue.) It is now time for the wise person to leave, and you thank him for coming to this, your own quiet place. You bid farewell, and watch the wise person leave and walk away into the distance. You then sit quietly in your quiet place and contemplate what the wise person has told you.

Other variations of this exercise are as follows:

Exercise 14

As you relax you imagine yourself standing in the centre of a field. Become fully present there in the centre of this field, and feel the warmth of the sun, the touch of the breeze on your cheek. Feel the fragrance, hear the sounds, and spend a moment really *feeling* yourself there in the field. As you look around the field you note on one side there is a mountain and your decide to climb the mountain. Visualise yourself crossing the field to the base of this mountain. Once there you choose to climb the mountain, and you begin to do so. The path you choose leads higher and higher, and you observe the vegetation as it changes the higher you ascend. Higher and higher you go up the mountain, until you sense you are near the top. As you reach the top of the mountain, there you see before you the figure of a wise person. You greet the wise person, and you sit and listen to what the wise person has to tell you. You are able to ask questions of the wise person, and you listen eagerly to what the wise person has to tell you. (Allow time for a full dialogue.) Now it is time to leave and you thank the wise person for being there, and turning, begin to make your way down the mountain once more. Further and further down you travel until eventually you find yourself back in the field. You make your way back to the centre of this field, and there you sit for a while contemplating your experience.

The following exercise presents a third way of making contact with the wise person.

Exercise 15

Once again find yourself standing in the centre of a field, and make that experience real for you. Feel the feelings, smell the smells, and fully experience yourself in the centre of your field. Once again you notice the mountain beside the field and you choose to climb the mountain. You follow the path, and steadily make your way to the top of the mountain. As you approach the top of the mountain you become aware of some form of construction. As you get closer you see what seems to be a temple. You slowly walk up to the entrance of the temple and pause there for a moment to study the structure. You feel drawn to enter the temple and gently do so. You move within the doorway and allow your eyes to accustom themselves to the dimmer light. As your eyes become accustomed to the gloom, you notice what seems to be an altar centrally situated in the temple. You move slowly towards this altar, and you are drawn to lie down on the altar itself. As you lie there you become open and receptive. You soon become aware of a figure approaching, the figure of a wise person dressed in robes. This figure greets you and your realise you are in the presence of a truly wise person. As you lie on the altar you hear what the wise person has to tell you about your life. Once again you are able to question the wise person, and receive his reply. It is time now for the wise person to leave, and you thank him for the advice he has given to you. You watch as he leaves the temple and gently you sit up and step down from the altar. Make your way slowly to the door of the temple, and move through into the sunlight beyond. Now gently make your way down the mountain, back to the centre of the field, and pause there for a while to contemplate your experience.

Visualisation for Pain Control

Pain is said to be the measure of the resistance we have in our system. It follows, therefore, that one of the first questions we should ask ourselves is 'What am I resisting?' 'Am I flowing with the flow, the stream of life, or am I fighting against the current?' 'Is there perhaps something I can change in my everyday life to alleviate the pain and suffering I am bringing on myself?'

Pain is a strange phenomenon. People involved in sport – especially contact sport – are often oblivious of pain until their attention is drawn to that area. Once they acknowledge the injury the pain begins. This does suggest that while we focus on the problem, or in this case the injury, we allow the pain to have power over us. If it looks bad it must be sore. Children are often oblivious of grazing a knee, for example, until they see the blood. At that point the tears pour out and the child cries for mummy to kiss it better! Have you noticed how quickly the pain disappears with mummy kissing it better? The act of kissing it better means the child no longer has to focus on that area, and it therefore no longer hurts. We are not suggesting that all pain can be relieved with a kiss or a change of focus, but we do suggest that there are ways of working with the pain that can make life easier.

In working with pain over the years we have found healing music to be most beneficial. As we discovered in the preceding part of this book, healing music tends to take the person from a left-brain focus on personality levels to right-brain transpersonal awareness. Healing music, in a sense, takes us out of ourselves. It allows us to dream, to float, to withdraw from the harsh reality of our present world. And the one piece of music that stands out above all the others in this field is *Cirrus* by John Richardson. *Cirrus* is used by Andrew Watson in dealing with all severe cases of pain, and even where people are approaching the death transition. One successful application was with a man who underwent major surgery for the removal of one kidney. As he became conscious after the operation earphones were placed on his head and *Cirrus* was played to him repeatedly. He needed virtually no pain killers, and was discharged on the fourth day after surgery.

It is important for each individual to find the best means of pain relief suited to their particular need. In the following visualisation we suggest one possible way of working with pain. We do not advocate that this will work in every case. It is purely a suggestion, and a point from which to develop your own method:

Exercise 16

For the purpose of this exercise we will assume that you have a pain in your head. The same method should be used for pain in any area of the body. We only use the head as a fairly common example.

Begin by focusing more clearly on the pain. Where exactly *is* the pain? Try and pinpoint it to the nearest millimetre. Is it three centimetres in from the left ear and 1½ centimetres higher, or where exactly is it situated? Having located the exact position of the source of the pain, now begin to look at the size of the pain. Is it round, or square? Is it jagged or smooth? What colour is it? Do you think it might have a particular fragrance, or perhaps even a taste? Having identified your pain more clearly in a physical sense, imagine now how your pain would feel if it were positioned elsewhere in the body. Spend a moment now and move the pain, for example, from the left side of your head to the right. How about we put the pain in your left shoulder, or perhaps your right knee? Spend a while experimenting with moving the pain from its present location. Imagine now putting that pain outside yourself. Really see the shape of the pain, see the colour, see the form, as being somewhere outside you. And then see the pain in whatever form you have given it disappear, move far away, and out of sight. This sequence should be repeated several times until the pain finally disappears.

Another way of working with pain is to give it form through the image. Once again presume you have a pain somewhere in your head. Begin now to get an image for that pain. What image or symbol comes to mind? Begin to see this image or symbol very clearly and set the image up in a position where you can have dialogue with it. Begin now by asking the image or the symbol why it is there. What are you doing in my head? And see what reply you get. By setting up a dialogue with the image you will be able to discover all about it, where it came from, why it's there, and what you can do to remove it. Very often the image will be there to get your attention. Ask it therefore what it needs from you. What can you do to allow it to leave? Presuming that there is something in your lifestyle or habit forms that created the pain in the first place, ask the image what you can change in your situation to help it. How can you make sure the pain does not return and keep bothering you? In what way do you need to express yourself to free that pain from your system?

Pain is not always the enemy. Pain is merely a symptom to say that there is something wrong. You will need, therefore, to take notice of the symptom. We need to stop for long enough to discover why the pain has occurred. By taking two aspirin tablets to relieve the headache you are purely removing the symptom. You have done nothing to determine the cause that created that pain in the first place. This is the underlying question we should ask ourselves in every health matter: 'Do we have a clear relationship with ourselves and with our environment?' For example, a healthy plant growing in its natural environment is never attacked by disease and exactly the same is true for people. Somewhere in your life you have gone off the rails! Until you can look at the underlying patterns in your life that have created the imbalance you will continue to suffer from time to time.

Healing music is fast becoming a therapeutic tool. More and more people around the world are using it to help them to relax and to find inspiration in their lives. By accessing so clearly our intuitive brain this music takes us out of the everyday, and allows us to introduce a transpersonal perspective to our lives. People who used to rely on hallucinogenic drugs to get the answers in their lives are now finding that a similar effect may be obtained by using this music to access the transpersonal. Not only is it better for you but it is also a lot cheaper!

6 THE RISE OF NEW AGE MUSIC

New Age Music is based on the idea that we can create music to alter our moods and expand our levels of awareness. Ironically, some of this music has its historical origins in the hedonistic and somewhat reckless psychedelic period of the late 1960's. Nowadays that era of hippies and flower-power may seem simplistic and indulgent, but there is no doubt that it was a time when large numbers of young people began to explore unfamiliar realms of consciousness and to experiment with new forms of art and creative expression.

It is really because of the widespread experimentation with psychedelic states that there was a renewal of interest in Eastern mysticism, Zen and such spiritual classics as the *I Ching* and *The Tibetan Book of the Dead*. People were tapping sacred energies from their unconscious minds and needed 'frameworks' to help them integrate their experiences. Around the same time the pioneering work of LSD researcher Dr John Lilly – who explored sensory isolation states – gave rise to the first prototypes of what we now know as flotation tanks: these days an accepted feature of the 'alternative' health scene.

So, in many ways the 1960's counter-culture was the forerunner of the present-day holistic health perspective. Similarly, New Age music has its roots in cosmic rock music, Indian ragas, meditative folk music and to a lesser extent, certain forms of contemporary jazz – for these sorts of music were popular with the 1960's counter-culture. Nowadays New Age music has become more bland and more mellow – especially to the extent that it is used for meditation and relaxation. Often it is even more 'minimal' than before, making widespread use of repeated cycles of gentle, undulating sounds.

In the following pages we trace the rise of New Age music in various regions of the world.

Britain

'Cosmic rock' developed in Britain in the late 1960's and early 1970's with the emergence of several new electronic rock groups, including Yes, King Crimson, Hawkwind, and The Moody Blues. However, the most distinctive of the new bands was undoubtedly Pink Floyd. After establishing themselves with *A Saucerful of Secrets* Pink Floyd issued the first of several classic albums, *Ummagumma*, in 1969. Recorded live, the double-album included such tracks as 'Astronomy Domine', 'Set the Controls for the Heart of the Sun' and 'Sysyphus', and featured expansive and sustained sequences of synthesiser and piano. Richard Wright's superb work on keyboards and organ was a highlight of the album and, perhaps for the first time in modern rock music, connections were being made – both in the lyrics and in the music – between the images of outer space and the inner worlds of consciousness. After the release in 1970 of *Atom Heart Mother*, characterised by both a sense of musical grandeur and also the special effects so much enjoyed by head-trippers, Pink Floyd went on to produce the album which stands out as one of their masterworks: *Meddle* (1971). Although the group still allowed lyrics to dominate on the first side of the album, the second side was devoted to an exquisite single composition. 'Echoes'. Largely instrumental, it featured beautiful sequences of vibrato synthesiser, evoking the textures of crystalline space. 'Echoes' concludes with a soaring and uplifting musical effects suggestive of astral projection – implying transformation to another plane of existence.

Although Pink Floyd could undoubtedly have developed the abstract, textural mode established on *Meddle* they chose not to. Their next album, *The Dark Side of the Moon*, brilliant and commercially successful though it was, once again made its impact through its lyrics, rather than through its music, and even included a type of warning:

'And if the dam breaks open many years too soon,
And if there is no room upon the hill,
And if your hand explores with dark forebodings too,
I'll see you on the dark side of the moon...'

This sense of hesitancy, perhaps even of paranoia, continued with *Wish You Were Here*. In 'Shine On You Crazy Diamond' vocalist Roger Waters' tone was ominous indeed:

'Now there's a look in your eyes,
Like black holes in the sky...
You reached for the moon – threatened
by shadows at night and exposed in the light...'

Such directions in the music of Pink Floyd have since taken an even more dramatic form – in the intense negativity and alienation of *The Wall* and on *The Final Cut*, which focuses on the hostility and senselessness of the Falklands War.

If Pink Floyd were major pioneers of cosmic rock – and they certainly influenced the important German group Tangerine Dream – they did not develop the pure, simplified style of synthesiser music which later emerged in Europe. For some time British rock music remained complex and diverse, and it was left to other musicians to develop the abstract qualities vital to inner space music.

The rival group King Crimson were a band who, like Pink Floyd, were capable of both richly layered compositions and exquisite simplicity. Their early albums, *In the Court of the Crimson King* and *In the Wake of Poseidon*, were mythic and grand in conception, and it was only on later releases like *Islands* that a simplified range of musical textures began to appear. The sensitivity of King Crimson, in large degree, was due to the creativity of its lead guitarist Robert Fripp who, after the group's fragmentation, went on to record several beautiful works both on his own and with other artists. On *Evening Star* (1975), for example, Fripp teamed with former Roxy Music member Brian Eno to produce one of the most delicate inner space albums ever recorded. Combining electric guitar and synthesiser, *Evening Star* featured the lovely abstract compositions 'Wind on Water', 'Wind on Wind' and 'Evensong'. However, by 1979 Fripp had reverted to a more raucous electronic style and was now paying more attention to lyrics. His solo album *Exposure* had seventeen tracks, only three of them *(Urban Landscape, Water Music I* and *Water Music II)* in the delicate instrumental style of the earlier album.

Fripp's colleague, Brian Eno, on the other hand, has since become Britain's leading exponent of 'minimal' electronic music. Although he has maintained close connections with contemporary rock idioms – as witnessed on his solo albums *Taking Tiger Mountain, Here Come the Warm Jets* and *Before and After Science*, and in his collaboration with Talking Heads – he has also produced some of the finest inner space compositions recorded to date.

In September 1975 Eno evolved a work called 'Discreet Music' by fusing two melody lines while occasionally modifying the timbre of his synthesiser. The effect was a subtle blend of what Eno calls 'gradual processes', resulting in music that was so minimal that it could either be listened to or ignored. Eno was in fact building towards his concept of 'ambience', which he later explained more fully in 1978 with the release of *Ambient One: Music for Airports*. By this stage Eno had become increasingly interested in 'environmental' music – a form he was keen to distinguish from the derivative and watered down mood music used in retail stores and other commercial environments. For Eno the task was to create a series of 'atmospheres' which could evoke a variety of moods. This was quite different from the purpose of 'muzak': 'Whereas the extant canned music companies proceed from the basis of regularising environments by blanketing their acoustic and atmospheric idiosyncrasies, Ambient Music is intended to enhance these. Whereas conventional background music is produced by stripping away all sense of doubt and uncertainty (and thus all genuine interest) from the music, Ambient Music retains these qualities. And whereas their intention is to 'brighten' the environment by adding stimulus to it (thus supposedly alleviating the tedium of routine tasks and levelling out the natural ups and downs of the body rhythms), Ambient Music is intended to induce calm and a space to think.'

Eno also emphasised the somewhat detached quality of his music: 'Ambient Music must be able to accommodate many levels of listening attention without reinforcing one in particular; it must be as ignorable as it is interesting.'

Music for Airports includes beautiful synthesiser and piano sequences and is simultaneously relaxing and engaging. It was followed in 1980 by *Ambient Two: The Plateaux of Mirror*. Here Eno worked with American musician Harold Budd on a series of compositions for piano and synthesiser. The music is at times crystalline, at times reflective, at times diffuse. The mind is free to build images from the sensitive and delicate changes in mood and tone and is lulled from one musical environment to the next. Eno's releases since then have included *Ambient Four: On Land* (1982) and *Apollo* (1983) – music composed to evoke the 'atmosphere' of the successful American space-landing on the moon. *Ambient Four* includes a variety of marsh, wind and beach sound-effects. The music for *Apollo*, on the other hand, captures the awesome mystery of space and the unique adventure of the astronauts. Eno was intrigued by the possibility that Alan Shepard and his colleagues could be experiencing 'a unique mixture of feelings that quite possibly no human had ever experienced before'.

The *Ambient* albums are important works in any catalogue of inner space music and have unquestionably set new standards in recorded synthesiser music. Other relevant works for meditation and imagery work can be found on Eno's *Possible Musics* (co-composed with Jon Hassell), on *Music for Films* (especially the three 'Sparrowfall' tracks), on *The Pearl*, *'Thursday Afternoon* and on *Another Green World* ('Becalmed').

Although Eno is now the dominant force in British inner space synthesiser music, he is not alone in his experimentation.

The British rock instrumentalists Jon Field and Tony Duhig, better known as Jade Warrior, recorded a series of albums in the 1970's featuring such musical instruments as harp, gong, glockenspiel, flute, drums, piano, guitar, organ and vibes. Jade Warrior's beautiful first album, *Floating World*, released in 1974, was dedicated to the Japanese philosophy of 'living only for the moment' and 'floating along the river current'. This was followed by *Waves* (1975), which included Steve Winwood on moog and piano, and *Kites* (1976) – an album which opens with musical impressions of a forest. Duhig and Field used tape-recorders to capture the mood of Nature 'as the sun comes up, the forest wakes and the wind begins to blow through the trees'. Subsequent tracks included compositions evoking the sense of floating in the wind, and music to accompany Zen stories attributed to Lu K'uan Yu.

Another musician to achieve major impact in the inner space genre is Mike Oldfield. Widely recognised for his evocative theme music for the feature film *The Exorcist*, included on the *Tubular Bells* album, Oldfield became known for his remarkable ability to master a wide range of instruments, including guitar, harp, bass, mandolin, bodhran, bazouki and piano. While his earliest recordings, *Tubular Bells* and *Hergist Ridge*, now seem a little dated, Oldfield's music can be exhilarating and powerful, sweeping the listener along with its often intricate melodies. In recent times, as evidenced on his albums *Five Miles Out* and *Crises*, Oldfield has begun to incorporate lyrics into his music – featuring such vocalists as Maggie Reilly and Jon Anderson – and because lyrics in general tend to intrude on a meditative state the latest albums have little interest for guided imagery work. However, several tracks from his middle-phase recordings *Ommadawn* (1975) and *Incantations* (1978) have exciting meditative possibilities.

In a quite separate development, and owing less to the cosmic rock music genre by way of influences, we have also seen a new musical movement in Britain which is distinctly meditative in emphasis.

In 1982, former naturopath and psychologist Colin Willcox formed a distribution company – New World Cassettes – to specifically focus on healing music: music created to relax, inspire and uplift its listeners. Over the next three years, Willcox contacted a range of musicians – some comparatively well known, others more obscure – and gradually developed a catalogue of some 150 releases.

Some of the musicians had a traditional musical training or background – Tim Wheater (*Awakenings, The Enchanter*) had performed with James Galway and the London Symphony Orchestra, while Chris Ashby (*Renaissance*) was a classical guitarist. Others like Arden Wilken (*Music for Healing, Inner Harmony*) – an American-born musician living in the Mediterranean – and John Richardson (*Cirrus, Spirit of the Redman*) were health therapists. Wilken teaches meditation and energy-balancing while Richardson is a herbalist, masseur and reflexologist with a clinic in Romford, Essex. Richardson says his music is used by 'fellow healers' in holistic health clinics, both at home and abroad, and also as backgrounds to meditation, yoga and tai chi.

Another well-known musician recording for New World is David Sun, a composer skilled both on keyboards and acoustic guitar. Sun's style is muted, abstract and gentle, and much of his music is suitable for Nature meditations. *The Secret Garden*, for example, includes bird songs, Nature sounds and acoustic strumming, while *Tranquility* presents Sun's talents as an ambient pianist. His recent release *Deep Enchantment* is an especially fine album of relaxation music.

Also on Willcox's label is the talented English synthesiser player Clifford White, who could well emerge as England's answer to Kitaro (see section on Japan). White's *Ascension* – one of the most accomplished of the New World releases – features a wide range of musical tones and textures. Strongly melodic, and therefore more useful for relaxation than specific visualisations, the album often has an orchestral quality, despite the fact that all of the effects were electronically created. 'Church of Light' is regal and most attractive, with its harp-like introduction and rich layers of synthesiser, while 'Hallowed Ground' is full of mystery – the music seems to rise up from the earth as if in awesome revelation. 'Ascension' itself is almost a type of 'Moonlight Sonata', and ethereal effects are added to give considerable depth to the composition.

To some extent Willcox's new label has taken the shine from the inner space music previously released on such labels as Virgin – which now features more commercial and mainstream acts like Boy George and Fearghal Sharkey. New World, on the other hand, features many completely new names – Chris Glassfield,

Karma, Mike Brooks, Thor Baldursson, Les Hurdle, Nicholas Land, Paul Fitzgerald, Mark Flanagan, Stairway and Michael Law – and it would seem that British New Age music is broadening its horizons. The New World catalogue is now being marketed internationally (see listings in Appendix A).

Europe

The development of inner space synthesiser music in Europe is primarily a German phenomenon dominated by Tangerine Dream and Klaus Schulze and other relatively less well known musicians like Yatha Sidhra, Michael Hoenig, Peter Michael Hamel, Cluster, Dzyan and Annexus Quam. However, the Swedish keyboards player Bo Hansson, Greek virtuoso Vangelis and Frenchman Jean-Michel Jarre have also made significant contributions. In general terms, while in Britain this form of electronic music has tended to become more simple after complex beginnings, the reverse has been true in Europe. Many of Tangerine Dream's earliest releases were expansive, uncluttered 'space music', while most of the recent albums have tended to promote more distinctive melody lines and heavier rhythms. The work of Jarre, Vangelis and also the Klaus Schulze protege Kitaro is similarly strong on melody while still retaining a fondness for abstract musical textures.

The earliest releases for the Berlin-based group Tangerine Dream remain classics of inner space music. The three-man group – which at that stage comprised Edgar Froese on electric guitar and generator, Chris Franke on synthesiser and cymbals, and Peter Baumann on synthesiser, organ and vibraphone – formed in 1965 and first played conventional rock music in the American style. They listened to the music of Pink Floyd but also to Liszt, Debussy, Wagner, Stockhausen, Ligeti and Sibelius, and were keen to push these musical forms towards a new frontier. Their early albums, *Alpha Centauri* (1971), *Zeit* (1972) and *Atem* (1972-3) retain a sense of romanticism but are very much expressions of space and texture. *Zeit*, for example, opens with cosmic synthesiser and a profound sense of emergence, as expressed in the title of the first track: 'Birth of Liquid Pleiades'. The music evokes the ever-gradual and time-encompassing process of the birth of stars in the universe, and bursts of electric organ seem to herald the possibility of life. On 'Nebulous Dawn' one can imagine light trickling over scarred rock-formations on a forgotten planet while 'Supernatural Probabilities' features unusual voice-like effects suggestive of a strange extra-terrestrial ritual performed by invisible gods.

Tangerine Dream developed this sense of mystery on their later albums *Phaedra* (1974) and *Rubycon* recorded, like all their subsequent releases, on the English Virgin label. *Phaedra*, named after the doomed daughter of King Minos of Crete, is an album of considerable beauty and dignity. Its second side, which is especially fine, opens with a passage suggestive of *Peer Gynt* and explores silken textures and ethereal forms in an extraordinary, undulating manner as the music seems to unfold from within itself, revealing new moods of expression. *Rubycon* is remarkable for the way in which the double moog synthesiser and organ are able to simulate the effects of inner space voices, capturing a sense of timelessness and awe found elsewhere perhaps only in the works of Ligeti.

As the group began to develop a popular following, Tangerine Dream now began to tour England, playing where possible not in concert halls or auditoriums but in the tranquil and sacred spaces offered by large cathedrals, for example in Coventry and Liverpool. Their audiences sat in total darkness, absorbing the mystery of the music.

Tangerine Dream, however, did not choose to sustain this unified direction in their music, and their next albums, *Ricochet* and *Stratosfear* were less consistent, despite individual compositions of interest. Signs of fragmentation began to appear and by January 1978 – when *Cyclone* was recorded – Peter Baumann had left the group and had been replaced by vocalist Steve Joliffe and percussionist Klaus Krieger. Baumann subsequently recorded two solo albums, *Romance 76* (1976) and *Trans Harmonic Nights* (1979). For the most part his music had less substance than the former work with Froese and Franke and, particularly on the later album, was inclined to be whimsical and melodic - anticipating a change of direction in European synthesiser music as a whole.

Edgar Froese, meanwhile, had recorded two evocative solo albums, *Aqua* (1973-4) and *Epsilon in Malaysian Pale* (1975), the former interesting for its watery effects and mysterious synthesiser sounds, the latter rich and romantic in the style already established by *Phaedra*. But he, too, now inclined towards more pronounced rhythms and melodies with the release of *Ages* in 1978 and *Stuntman* in 1979. Some of the tracks on *Ages*, for example 'Metropolis' and 'Nights of Automatic Women', are urgent and aggressive while 'Icarus' offers a basic three-chord riff similar to Booker T & the MG's rhythm and blues instrumental 'Green Onions'. Simple melody lines dominate on 'Golgotha and the Circle Closes' and 'Ode to Granny A'. Similarly, on *Stuntman*, although 'Scarlet Score for Mescalero' is sumptuous and expansive, the title track offers an electronic melody line simulating Spanish trumpets.

The recent releases of Tangerine Dream are of mixed value for guided imagery work. *Force Majeure* is perhaps their most impressive album in the last five years, featuring unusual percussive effects and lilting synthesiser rhythms. On the other hand, while both *Tangram* (1980) and *Logos* (1981) have the advantage of continuous tracks on both sides, making extended visualisation easier, both albums suffer slightly from rhythmic intrusions that break the mood. *Tangram* is evocative and haunting nevertheless, and *Logos* similarly presents a subtle and reflective quality despite the fact that it was recorded live (at the Dominion, London). *White*

Eagle (1982), on the other hand, may prove to be a crossroads for the group. Drawing on the imagery of the American Indian, it offers both gimmicky and whimsical tracks like 'Convention of the 24' and 'White Eagle', as well as more abstract music with a sense of expectancy ('Mojave Plan').

While Tangerine Dream emerged as a powerful musical force in Berlin, another important group had also formed: Ash Ra Tempel. This group did not survive for long as a single entity but two of its members, keyboards player Klaus Schulze and guitarist Manuel Gottsching, have since emerged in their own right as solo performers.

The 1972 release *Join Inn* shows that Ash Ra Tempel had their roots in orthodox rock'n roll. However, the lengthy instrumental 'Jenseits' on the second side had an exquisite, eerie quality characteristic of early German inner space music. In the same year as *Join Inn*, Schulze released the first of his many solo albums, *Irrlicht*. While it certainly revealed the potential of his late work the album was distant and uncommitted, offering a surprising, and somewhat unsatisfactory blend of church organ monotone and musical textures that sounded like weather effects. *Cyborg*, recorded in 1973 with an elaborate 'Cosmic Orchestra', was more interesting, opening with a carefully layered theme. The second track, 'Conphara', offered rich velvet tones while on 'Chromengel' Schulze interposed his synthesiser with the cello and strings instrumentation of the orchestra, producing a curious high-pitched vibrato. Schulze's best work, however, still lay ahead. *Blackdance* was recorded in 1974 for Metronome and showed the musician's superb facility on synthesiser, organ, piano, percussion and guitar. 'Ways of Changes' merges synthesiser with gentle, acoustic guitar, and there is a sustained rhythm as waves of electronic sound break overhead, like surf over rocks. 'Some Velvet Phasing' shows the muted and dignified side of Schulze's music, while 'Voices of Syn', which makes use of Ernst Walter Siemen's bass chanting, adds a strange pagan quality to the electric organ.

Timewind (1975) produced a new direction altogether: the music was crisp, vibrant and metallic and included unusual humming effects superimposed over steady bass rhythms. At times the textures of the music were misty and rarefied, and at other times rich and deep. 'Bayreuth Return' is especially magical, and although it is dedicated to Wagner it provides more the impression of a shaman's spirit-catcher whirling in the air!

Schulze's next releases, *Moondawn* (1976) and *Mirage* (1977), have similarly established themselves as important inner space albums,. 'Floating', the first side of *Moondawn*, features delicate synthesiser sequences and muted rhythm effects while the first half of 'Mindphaser' is ethereal and uplifting. *Mirage*, with its classic composition 'Crystal Lake', remains one of the masterpieces of the genre, and its lilting synthesiser rhythms provide an ideal musical medium for guided imagery.

While the 1977 film soundtrack *Body Love* was less varied than his earlier releases Klaus Schulze produced a fine double album, *X*, in 1979, and has demonstrated with his recent releases *Trancefer* (1981) and *Audentity* (1983) that he is still capable of impressive and imaginative work. Both of these albums have potential application in guided imagery visualisation. *Trancefer* includes sequences where tactile rhythms are incorporated with sounds reminiscent of chanting. 'Silent Running' on the second side, builds from a gentle opening to a well sustained rhythmic tempo, and the tapping effects provide the music with a primitive shamanic quality. And while the double album *Audentity* is at times discordant and hesitant, it too has rich possibilities. 'Armourage' on Side Two begins with echoey, cavernous effects, transforming from subterranean watery impressions to the texture of air, while 'Sebastian im Traum' offers eerie, melancholy effects similarly suggestive of water and caves. 'Spielglocken' is a type of synthesiser raga whose pace builds gradually, and it too allows a range of musical textures for visualisation. Interestingly, Schulze conceived this work as an expression of the search for self-identity, exploring the impressions and associations provided by his music. As Garry Havrillay writes on the accompanying sleeve notes, 'Voices call from the future and past, doors open and close, dominating his thoughts, reviewing, and evaluating... There are reflections which menace... like insects writhing in the brain, then moments of solitude, some of which are isolated with apprehension and others with serenity'. It is precisely this richness of tonal colour and mood that makes the music useful for guided imagery.

Manuel Gottsching has been less prolific than Klaus Schulze but nevertheless similarly experimental. His individual albums include *Inventions for Electrical Guitar*, recorded in Berlin in 1974, and as Ash Ra, *New Age of Earth* (1976) and *Blackouts* (1977). As a guitarist and synthesiser musician Gottsching inclines towards fully developed rhythmic compositions and as a whole his work lacks Schulze's subtlety. However, specific works like 'Ocean of Tenderness' and 'Quasarsphere' are central to the inner space genre.

Other German musicians who have produced interesting and experimental work include Michael Hoenig and Peter Michael Hamel. Hoenig was born in Hamburg and studied journalism and theatre at Berlin's Free University. After becoming interested in free-form music in 1968 he began to experiment with electronic sounds and assisted Klaus Schulze in recording *Timewind*. He later toured Australia and England with Tangerine Dream. His solo album *Departure from the Northern Wasteland*, released in 1978, features several fine synthesiser tracks, including 'Hanging Garden Transfer' and 'Voices of Where' – both of which have evocative, abstract qualities. More recently Hoenig has assisted Philip Glass in creating music for the soundtrack of the remarkable film *Koyaanisqatsi*.

Peter Michael Hamel has also had a distinguished musical career and is also the author of the important book *Through Music to the Self*, first published in 1976. After studying composition with Fritz Buechtger and Guenter Bialas at the Music Academy in Munich, he began to compose music for stage, television and opera and has since received several awards for his music, including the Villa Massimo Rome Prize in 1980. A devotee of Indian music, he became strongly involved with meditative styles of composition, especially music featuring a stable pulse and 'modular' structure. Hamel's Indian influence is demonstrated on *The Voice of Silence* and his album with the group Between, *Dharana*, recorded with a symphony orchestra. Another of his albums *Colours of Time*, released in 1980, features meditative synthesiser music based on the cyclic, 'modular' style.

As we mentioned earlier, the contemporary European synthesiser musicians these days incline more towards melody than abstract texture. Jean-Michel Jarre achieved international recognition for his albums *Oxygene* and *Equinoxe* and passages from this music have proved suitable for feature films. Similarly Vangelis' *Chariots of Fire* and *Ignacio* were both composed with the requirements of the film medium in mind. Consequently, although this type of electronic music has undoubted evocative qualities it tends to be fragmented and diverse in approach and usually does not extend sufficiently, either in length or mood, to allow a practical application in guided imagery work. It also has the disadvantage, from a meditative viewpoint, of bringing to mind specific image-associations from the film with which it is associated. In the same way, Bo Hansson's electronic albums *Music Inspired by Lord of the Rings* and *Music Inspired by Watership Down* also have limited meditative application because they are related to individual literary works and likewise tend to stimulate specific memory associations rather than archetypal processes in the imagination.

The United States

Contemporary American music encompasses a number of traditions, including the many facets of classical and electronic music, jazz, blues, folk and rock. Not surprisingly the inner space and meditative music which has emerged from the United States has a number of divergent sources. The jazz of John and Alice Coltrane, the guitar music of rock artist Devadip Carlos Santana, the piano of Keith Jarrett and the experimental music of Philip Glass, Steve Reich, La Monte Young and Terry Riley – all of these, at different times and for different listeners, could be said to have meditative qualities. There is also the distinct genre of relaxation music – associated with the work of Steven Halpern and other west-coast musicians – as well as the idiosyncratic blend of musical styles created at the ashram of guru Bhagwan Shree Rajneesh during his stay in Oregon. And across the border, Canadian-based New Yorker Paul Horn has produced several beautiful albums of meditative flute music inspired by the Great Pyramid and the Taj Mahal.

Of the new wave musicians, American composer Philip Glass is currently among the most prominent. A winner of Ford Foundation and Fulbright grants for his modular form of music, Glass achieved recognition for his *Music in 12 Parts* (1974) and his operas *Einstein on the Beach* (1976) and *Satyagraha* (1980). He has recently been acclaimed for the remarkable music he has written for the impressionistic film *Koyaanisqatsi* – a unique visual sequence of landscapes and urban images. The music itself is often hypnotic and trance-inducing, and features some unforgettable deep chanting.

Terry Riley is also one of the most influential of the new wave musicians and established his 'modal' and 'cyclic' styles prior to the advent of inner space music in Europe. Born in California in 1935, he studied music in San Francisco and went to Europe in 1962, performing as far afield as France and Scandinavia. From a meditative viewpoint, Riley's album *Rainbow in Curved Air*, recorded in 1969, remains his most significant, although *Persian Surgery Dervishes* and *Happy Ending* – released in Europe in the 1970s – earned him an enthusiastic following. In 1980 Riley released *Shri Camel*, a work which had originally been commissioned by Radio Bremen in early 1975. Riley used an elaborate digital delay system to enable him to play duets and trios as an accompaniment to the solo, and to experiment with electronic acoustics. Unfortunately the work suffers from a pronounced heaviness of tone and at times is surprisingly discordant. 'Anthem of the Trinity' seems rather heavy-handed by comparison with the dextrous facility of Klaus Schulze, and 'Celestial Valley' appears to lose direction mid-way. 'Across the Lake of the Ancient Word' and 'Desert of Ice' are perhaps the most successful tracks, showing Riley's virtuosity on keyboards and allowing more spontaneity and freshness in the music.

A far more successful album, from a meditative or 'spiritual' point of view, is Geoffrey Chandler's *Starscapes*, released on the Californian Unity label in 1980. Chandler's music has been accurately described as 'environmental, meditative, transporting and romantic' and at its best can be aptly compared to the most subtle work of Tangerine Dream on *Zeit* and Klaus Schulze on *Moondawn*. Resonant, ethereal and delicate, it is one of the most beautiful inner space albums yet released in the United States.

Other serene and gentle musical works have been issued on cassette (and occasionally on record) by small Californian music companies and are not always easily obtainable. They include music by flautist and zither player Schawkie Roth, the vibraphone and piano compositions of Jon Bernoff and Marcus Allen, the *Golden Voyage* series of Robert Bearns and Ron Dexter and the exquisite *Inner Sanctum* recording of Aeoliah and Larkin. Aeoliah, a German visionary artist and synthesiser musician, combined on this tape with Californian moog-player Don Robertson and the sensitive flautist Larkin, and the result is one of the most beautiful and transcendental inner space compositions yet produced. Larkin has also issued several other fine recordings, including *To the Essence of a Candle*, *O'cean*, and *Concert Journey*.

Allied to this genre is the work of Steven Halpern whose music has been developed specifically for relaxation and self-healing. Halpern did not always play the gentle and sensual music he has become famous for. Originally a trumpeter and guitarist, he gravitated to jazz while studying sociology at the University of Buffalo and was initially influenced by such musicians as saxophonist Archie Shepp and drummer/pianist Joe Chambers. However, Zen and the works of Gurdjieff were fashionable subjects on the campus at the time and Halpern became increasingly interested in mysticism. Some years later, while he was meditating in the woods near Santa Cruz, his perspective in this area deepened. 'I started hearing this gently flowing music', he recalls. 'Basically I heard what became my album *Spectrum Suite* in a couple of seconds.' He walked down the road to a nearby growth centre – 'a kind of mini Esalen' – and began to play on the piano. The music needed developing but the essential ingredients were there. 'Since I had never studied piano,' Halpern says, 'I was working more from sounds that I would hear – phrases and harmonic and melodic combinations.'

Halpern's recent music is delicate and tranquil and tends at times towards blandness. The understated quality, however, is deliberate. Halpern's main aim is to produce music which is therapeutic and he believes that to produce the 'relaxation response' all semblance of a regular beat should be removed. This leaves spaces between the musical phrases and allows the meditative mood to develop – thereby increasing the alpha brain-wave pattern in the consciousness of the listener.

Halpern is a prolific musician and it is not easy to know where to start when presented with a range of his attractively packaged cassettes. Among his best recordings are *Zodiac Suite*, a work combining piano, violin, zither and flutes; *Spectrum Suite*, a solo album which links the seven notes of the musical octave to the seven colours of the visual spectrum, and *Eventide*, which evokes feelings of stillness and peace.

Also offered as meditation music, but often more exuberant and colourful than that, are the diverse musical compositions of the now semi-defunct Rajneesh Foundation. Bhagwan noted in his discourse *Music the Ultimate Meditation* that music can create harmony both in our environment and also within each one of us. Accordingly he encouraged the development of meditation music at his former ashrams in Poona and Oregon. While it is not as well recorded as its European counterparts, it nevertheless presents a sense of vitality and joy.

The best known of the Rajneesh musicians is German-born Swami Chaitanya (Georg Deuter), who recorded his early albums at Poona and later in California. His philosophy of life is a meditative one and consists of 'relating peace, beauty, balance and joy through music'.

Aum was Deuter's first album of meditative music and it included a mix of acoustic instruments, synthesiser and the sounds of the sea. A blend of relaxed moods and rhythmic composition, it is less satisfying than some of his later albums. He followed it with *Celebration*, featuring bells, bird sounds and vibrant guitar strumming, and the beautiful *Ecstasy*, with its evocative flute and guitar. *Haleakala*, inspired by a Hawaiian volcano also known as the House of the Sun, blended vocals with zither, flute, synthesiser and piano, and the often delicate *Silence is the Answer* evoked an Eastern ambience with synthesiser, recorder, guitar and percussion. His more recent release *Nirvana Road* – perhaps his best album so far – featured vibrant celebratory music in the style of Gheorge Zamfir and Mike Oldfield.

While Deuter was undoubtedly the most visible of the Rajneesh Foundation musicians, fellow *sannyasin* Swami Govinddas was also impressive and there were a number of recordings where individual performers were not identified – suggesting that there were many unrecognised musicians of great talent at Rajneeshpuram. Among the best of these releases – and they are still available, despite the demise of the Oregon ashram – are Swami Chaitanya's *Flowers of Silence*, Swami Govinddas' *Just a Glimpse* and the anonymous compositions *Nataraj* and *Nadabrahma*. *Flowers of Silence* features guitar, recorder, shakuhachi, synthesiser and tablas and has some beautiful moments, especially when the recorder comes to the fore. There are also chime effects and classically inspired sequences of acoustic guitar. *Just a Glimpse* similarly offers a diverse range of musical instruments including guitar, mandolin, tambura, sitar and zither, blending western folk music styles with the traditional Indian *raga*. Neither of these is strictly meditational however: *Flowers of Silence* at times evokes a Renaissance atmosphere, and *Just a Glimpse* offers a variety of moods and melodies.

Nataraj and *Nadabrahma*, by contrast, are altogether different. The first of these is written for an exuberant meditation style which divides into three parts. The first, lasting 40 minutes, includes a meditation-dance of total frenzy in which the unconscious mind is encouraged to 'take over completely'. This is followed by 20 minutes of stillness and calm, culminating in five minutes of 'celebration and joy'.

Nadabrahma is composed to accompany an ancient Tibetan meditation technique usually performed either at night or in the early hours of the morning. For the first 30 minutes the practitioner sits relaxed and visualises the body as a hollow vessel. Humming sounds are made in unison with the music. After this the hands are rotated in large outward circles with the palms facing up. Later the palms are faced down and the hands are moved in an inward circular motion toward the body. The meditation ends with a period of silence. The music itself is spacey and cavernous – seeming to flow from the very centre of the earth. Consisting of dark, deep tonal colours, it is for the most part slow and intense, although towards the close it becomes more spirited – as if the soul were freed from its constrictions.

Finally, in summarising some of the main directions of American meditation music mention should be made of Paul Horn's superb flute compositions, Herbie Mann's musical exploration of traditional Japanese art-forms, Henry Wolff and Nancy Hennings' compositions for Tibetan bells, and the unique music of Ray Lynch.

Horn is best known for his two albums *Inside* and *Inside the Great Pyramid*. The first of these was recorded in 1968 on location in the Taj Mahal – specifically in the central dome which houses the bodies of Shah Jahan and Mumtaz Mahal. Horn found that the dome had remarkable acoustic properties; when an Indian guard called out suddenly the tone and texture of his voice seemed to remain suspended in the air, with voice and echo blending into one. Horn was inspired by the magical atmosphere of the Taj Mahal and recorded several very beautiful compositions there with the permission of the guard – including 'Mantra 1' and 'Vibrations'.

Later, in 1976, Horn was invited to visit Egypt with an archaeological team. Several members of the group were interested in examining the Pyramids in terms of 'meditative vibrations', resonances and energy fields. Horn was most impressed by the famous King's Chamber in the Great Pyramid – a majestic room some 34 feet long and 19 feet high, with a ceiling of polished red granite. Awed by the sanctity of the environment, he felt, as he says in his own words, 'a strong spiritual force or energy permeating the atmosphere and simply responded to it'. His recordings there, and also in the Queen's Chamber and in the Kephren Pyramid burial chamber, are masterpieces of meditative flute playing.

American flautist Herbie Mann is usually associated with more mainstream jazz music but he made something of an obscure musical detour in the mid 1970s to explore the textural qualities of Japanese *gagaku* and *shomyo* music. The *gagaku* form of instrumental music dates from the 8th century and has Chinese, Indian and Korean origins. *Shomyo* is a type of Buddhist chant that gained ascendancy in the 11th century and has parallels with the Western Gregorian style. In 1976 Mann took his jazz group to Tokyo and recorded *Gagaku & Beyond*, an impressionistic jazz album that includes a *shomyo* chant, the traditional *shakuhachi* and *koto*, and also the less familiar *sho* mouth organ, *taiko* drum and *samisen* stringed instrument. Because the music derives from a profound spiritual source it has remarkable meditative and guided imagery possibilities and represents, for Mann, 'the expansion of both Eastern and Western ideals'.

Avant-garde musicians Henry Wolff and Nancy Hennings have similarly turned to the East for their mystical expression using only Tibetan bells. Their music is ethereal and timeless, often sounding like electronic inner space music despite its much simpler folk-origins. When Wolff and Hennings performed before the *karmapa*, or leader of a Tibetan Buddhist monastery in Sikkim, he declared the music to be 'the sound of the Void', and indeed it captures a uniquely mysterious quality not found elsewhere in the genre.

The first album of music, titled simply *Tibetan Bells*, was recorded in 1971 and was very much the prototype for *Tibetan Bells II*, released a decade later. On the more recent album, the beautiful resonances of the bells are used to conjure a musical atmosphere appropriate to the *Bardo* visions experienced at death and described in the *Tibetan Book of the Dead*. The album opens with music depicting the severance of the spirit from the body and progresses with compositions relating to the soul's journey on the inner planes. It culminates with a sequence in which, to quote Henry Wolff, 'in its transcendent aspect of pure, abstract vibration, Spirit sets out on its final journey through the Void, across the vast expanse of the universe'.

The music of Ray Lynch is distinctive in another way. It too has a mystical orientation – the American spiritual teacher Da Free John has been a major influence on his work – but it also has a joyous, spontaneous quality that gives the music special appeal.

Trained in classical guitar and music theory, Lynch studied composition at the University of Texas and played lute with the Renaissance Quartet. He has released two New Age albums to date: *The Sky of Mind* (1983) and *Deep Breakfast* (1985).

The Sky of Mind featured a wide range of instruments, including synthesiser, piano, guitar, Tibetan bells, flute, recorder, cello and violin. The album is essentially a modern interpretation of classical and folk themes. *Deep Breakfast*, however, was altogether different from the first album. Several of the tracks were whimsical and light-hearted while others – featured beautiful viola and lute, and reflected the artist's Renaissance interests.

Because of its wide range of cultural and musical traditions, the United States has produced what is undoubtedly the most diverse range of New Age music. The flow of new releases from California has, however, eased somewhat, and the impetus now seems to rest with individual musicians, like Lynch, who are scattered around the country. These artists are intent on producing their own distinctive works, usually on specialist or minority labels. Recording quality has steadily increased, though, and many of the albums, including *Deep Breakfast*, are impeccably recorded.

Japan

Japan is represented in the New Age genre by master musician Masanori Takashi, otherwise known as Kitaro.

Born in 1953 in Toyohashi City in the Aichi prefecture, Kitaro graduated from high school and formed a rock group – the Far Eastern Family Band. He was already playing bass, keyboards and a variety of other instruments. In 1974 FEFB had a Japanese hit record with 'Theory of Hollow Earth' and the group began to attract a cult following on the American West Coast.

Two years earlier Kitaro had gone to Europe, and there he had met the German synthesiser musicians Klaus Schulze and Georg Deuter. Kitaro was impressed by the way both men brought a spiritual quality to their music and says that both had a profound influence on him. Kitaro subsequently travelled to India, Nepal, Tibet and Thailand and developed a strong interest in yoga and Zen Buddhism. His personal meditation experiences added a deeper dimension to his music.

Kitaro now began living like a recluse in a cave overlooking the Pacific Ocean, a short distance away from a small fishing village. However, the modest success of his early New Age recordings *Tenkai* (1978) and *Daichi* (1979) drew him back to civilisation and led to his first symphonic concert in Tokyo in September 1979. Performing in the Small Hall of the Kosei Nenkin Kaikan in Shinjuku, Kitaro played a synthesiser which could accommodate the sounds of 40 musical instruments – a world first.

Kitaro's album *Oasis* was released in Germany a month later and became one of his most successful international recordings. Meanwhile, in 1980, he was commissioned by NHK-TV to produce soundtracks for their epic series on the trade routes from China to Rome. This music was subsequently released on the three *Silk Road* albums which have also remained among his most popular.

In September 1980 Kitaro gave his first live concert – 'Kitaro in Person' – at the influential Parco-Seibu theatre in Shibuya, Tokyo. Later he was asked to record a special orchestral version of *Silk Road* with the London Symphony Orchestra – a type of sequel to Mike Oldfield's orchestral rendition of *Tubular Bells*.

Since then Kitaro has been in great demand to provide music for film soundtracks and to appear in live television concerts. Kitaro says of his music that it should not be considered intellectually, for it flows from his personal religious experiences, and his own inner condition plays a vital role in his musical creativity. 'My music,' he said in an interview in 1982, 'is somewhat different from the sound of Nature's movements, for it has positive love added. Furthermore, there is no self-oblivion or self-intoxication incorporated in my music, as is the case of Indian music – as represented by the sitar.'

Indeed, Kitaro's music is not strictly meditation music at all, despite the religious nature of its inspiration. The development of pronounced melody lines makes it less suitable for visualisation than the more abstract, minimal music of say, Brian Eno, but it is often profoundly uplifting and has a moving spiritual quality that is both optimistic and reassuring. Kitaro's *Silver Cloud*, released in 1983, is an excellent introduction to his mature work.

Australia and New Zealand

New Age music in Australasia is a comparatively recent development but is becoming increasingly sophisticated. While recording quality was originally a problem, many of the best releases are now indistinguishable from American and European recordings in terms of high production standards.

The names which stand out in New Age music from this region include Japetus, Ken Davis and Malcolm Harrison. Newcomers Alan Hinde, Jonathan Daemion and David Parsons have also produced excellent recordings in this genre.

Like Tangerine Dream in Germany, Japetus – whose real name is Jay Moxham – was strongly influenced by Pink Floyd. A self-taught musician, he learned to play keyboards, acoustic guitar and drums, and in 1982 built an 8-track recording studio. Influenced by a psychic named Ari Powell, he began to practise meditation and to study energy, auras and the spiritual symbolism of colours.

In 1984 Japetus released his first cassette of New Age music, *The Great, Great Silence*. Side One opens with a fine sense of expectation – the synthesiser is muted and delicate and the intention is to help the meditator explore different realms of consciousness. The music then 'lifts' through different chakra levels, taking the listener into higher levels of consciousness. Side Two begins with soaring, urgent sounds which soon give way to a sense of tranquillity. This particular music resembles Klaus Schulze's early compositions, and explores steady, undulating rhythms.

The following year Jepetus released *Once Around the Sun*, conceived, as he put it, 'to capture the grandeur of the planet circling the sun in a seasonal framework melded with the theme of the life, death and rebirth of its inhabitants.' He followed this with three cassettes commissioned by Bauer Verlag in West Germany to accompany Nevill Drury's *Musik Pforte zum Selbst, Brucke zum Kosmos* (English edition: *Music for Inner Space*). Here Japetus created specific sequences of music to accompany visualisations based on the major esoteric traditions: the Kabbalah, Astrology, the Tarot, Kundalini Yoga and *The Egyptian Book of the Dead*.

Then in November 1986, Japetus issued what is arguably his most impressive album to date – *Visions of Paradise* – inspired by, and composed for, the International Year of Peace. Side One features fleeting harps, soaring strings and interwoven melodies and there are also hints of choirs and lilting Indian rhythms. Side Two, however, was intended, as Japetus puts it, to 'take on more form and movement. A droplet becomes a cascade. A cascade becomes a river and the river empties into a sea of bliss. A swirling sheen of whispering voices ebb and flow with delicate flute and guitar. Finally, a gentle and melodic piece takes you dancing with the crystals'.

Perhaps the best New Age album released in Australia so far, *Visions of Paradise* is strongly reminiscent of Kitaro, although Japetus says he was unaware of Kitaro's music and developed his sound-textures independently.

Synthesiser player Ken Davis has only recently begun to record meditation music but as a performer he has been on the circuit since forming the group IQ in 1979 Davis' first release was the IQ *Mini Album* in 1982, featuring a Fairlight CMI synthesiser. His more recent productions include *Imagination* (1984), two 1985 releases *Visual Dreams* and *Feelings from Within*, and his more recent recordings *The Dawning of the New Age, Spirit of the Rainbow* and *Celestial Journey. Imagination* featured pulse and wave effects and seemed inspired by Baroque and Romantic music, while *Visual Dreams* – a less integrated album – combined exotic arabesque melodies with uptempo dance rhythms and lyrical piano sequences. *Feelings from Within*, on the other hand, was very much in the New Age genre, opening with sea-wave effects and the sounds of mewing seagulls.

Davis' more recent albums are mellow. Among the best is *Celestial Journey*, an ambient recording intended to soothe stress and assist total relaxation.

The music of Malcolm Harrison is more melodic than that of both Japetus and Davis, and to some extent links this musician more with the European style of New Age composition. This is not surprising, because Malcolm Harrison was born in England and grew up in a musical family. A former co-ordinator of the Paddington Healing and Growth Centre in Sydney, Harrison is equally adept at piano, synthesiser and acoustic guitar, as demonstrated on his album *Freefall* (1985). The music is characterised by crystalline piano, pulsing synthesiser and interesting changes of mood – from gentle to vibrant. On 'Sky Castles', the musician opens with acoustic guitar and then leads into piano and strings. The music has a haunting, evocative quality – like memories floating by in the wind. 'Adventures of a Snowflake', meanwhile, opens with delicate piano and builds a pattern of crisp and expressive melody lines over some mysterious chanting – an attractive and intriguing combination.

Mention should also be made here of Alan Hinde, Jonathan Daemion and New Zealander David Parsons, for they too have made worthwhile offerings in the New Age genre.

Alan Hinde studied piano and viola at the Canberra School of Music and then, in 1984, began using a synthesiser. He was already interested in relaxation and healing and developed his composition *The Twilight of Dreams* specifically as an aid to meditation. Utilising a Yamaha DX7 synthesiser, the music on this cassette is reminiscent of Steven Halpern's style of non-intrusive ambient music.

Jonathan Daemion is a Californian-born therapist who has lived in Australia for many years. A group-process facilitator who has worked in psychology, yoga, healing and meditation, Daemion is also a distinguished synthesiser musician and has released three recordings, *Mele, Robynsong* and *Tiki Sky: A Gift of Life.* Of these *Mele* is perhaps the most appealing – ideal music for healing, meditation and massage.

In New Zealand, David Parsons gained widespread recognition for his distinctive album *Sounds of Mothership*, recorded for Sun Energy Music. On this particular release Parsons blended classical Indian instruments with synthesiser and bird sounds – a meditative musical journey of some 90 minutes' duration. His more recent release, *Tibetan Plateau*, features synthesiser, vocoder, tamboura, piano, zither and Nature sounds. There are episodes of ethereal chanting and strains of cosmic organ which eventually dissolve into a long, extended meditation. Parsons releases his albums through a type of co-operative which also distributes the music of such New Age composers as Moana, the guitarist Divyanand, keyboards and 12-string guitarist Garth, and synthesiser musician Johnny Pepper. The aim of this group of artists is to heal and relax through their music, and in a collective statement the musicians put forward their credo: 'We believe that living in harmony with one's self and one's environment brings community and global co-operation and friendship.

One could hardly find a more succinct and evocative expression of the holistic philosophy than that!

APPENDIX A: DESCRIPTIONS OF ALBUMS USEFUL FOR CREATIVE VISUALISATION

Aeoliah. *The Light of Tao.* (Sona Gaia Productions)

Aeoliah is something of a mystery, for he has received very little publicity despite his extraordinary musical talents. A German visionary artist and synthesiser musician, he played alongside the distinguished flautist Larkin on the superb recording *Inner Sanctum* (1981) and has brought together a wide range of musicians on *The Light of Tao.* The variety of instruments is nothing less than dazzling: Aeoliah on synthesiser, zither, sitar, tamboura, chimes, cheng and piano; Donny Smith on electric guitar, Kip Setchko on flute, Dallas Smith on lyricon, and Jean St Laurent on harp.

The music is very much guided by an overriding spiritual philosophy and 'The Light of Tao' itself, which opens the album, suggests simultaneously both the diversity of life-forms and their underlying unity. Aeoliah discusses this in the accompanying sleeve notes:

'The flow of Nature,' he writes, 'lives and breathes all forms of life. As you hear the music, feel the pulse of life emanate from the celestial into the elemental kingdom, merging into pulsating waves of ecstatic union between Spirit and Nature...'

The title track opens with flute that wafts over mellow synthesiser. At times the synthesiser builds up into a chain of ethereal voices and the composition closes with the sound of crashing waves and the peal of chimes. 'Feather's River', which follows, begins in a rather different way, with vibratory rhythms and synthesiser very much in the style of Harold Budd and Brian Eno (*The Pearl, The Plateaux of Mirror*). Flute and harp are then introduced, increasing the rich timbre of the music.

Side Two, however, is the real highlight of the album, for the music here has a rapturous, blissful quality that is simply extraordinary. It is music, as Dr John Lilly would say, from a very high space indeed.

'Tien Fu: Heaven's Gate' features gently pulsing synthesiser and harp which creates a sense of exquisite expectancy. Electrical guitar is then introduced and merges beautifully with the flow. 'Mahavira', though, is the best track of all. Here Aeoliah opens with synthesiser to create the sacred sounds of inner space – music which seems to rise up in tribute to the vast span of the heavens. Sitar is then employed in a remarkable manner that is both evocative and worshipful. 'Mahavira' has wonderful dignity and adds a very mystical dimension to the music as a whole.

The Light of Tao is very special indeed and emerges as one of the finest ambient releases in recent years.

Christofer Ashby *Renaissance* (New World)
This beautiful and rather 'classical' recording features Chris Ashby on 6 and 12-string guitar and Tibetan bells, Laurie Baefsky on flute and Holly Bavmes on viola and violin.

Ashby has toured extensively in the United States and Europe and is a most accomplished guitarist. His album includes renditions of Pachelbel's 'Canon', J.S. Bach's 'Sicilenne', Debussy's 'Reverie' and Poulenc's 'Savabande', as well as an original composition, 'Byrd of Paradise'. There is certainly something here for New Age enthusiasts who also like John Williams and Julian Bream.

Mike Brooks *Fragile Shoreline* (New World)
Fragile Shoreline paints the power, the serenity, the vigour, the sensitivity of Nature. It is a supreme and majestic offering to the Elements, a work of intense feeling and brilliant originality, reminding us of the fragile beauty of our planet. The strength and power of the ocean is matched with its ethereal timeless and incalculable depths.

Harold Budd and Brian Eno *The Pearl* (Polygram)
Any album from Brian Eno is a welcome event. A very varied musician, his spectrum has ranged from mainstream and avant-garde rock with Roxy Music and Talking Heads through to the 'ambient' style for which he has become renowned.

Eno's best solo albums in the meditative mode include *Discreet Music, Music for Airports* and *Apollo* and he also produced an earlier work with Harold Budd titled *The Plateaux of Mirror* – a wonderful album of crystalline, ethereal music. On that record, as on this one, Budd collaborated with Eno at the Daniel Lanois studio in Ontario – with Budd on acoustic and electric piano and Eno on synthesiser and 'effects'.

Budd tends towards a complex piano style – he showed that on his solo album *The Pavilion of Dreams* – but his work with Eno is more muted. Here, with the exception of a track titled, 'A Stream With Bright Fish' where he is quite exuberant, Budd's approach is understated and introspective. There are, as usual, some very beautiful meditative tracks. 'The Silver Ball' is simply exquisite and so too are 'Their Memories' and the title track 'The Pearl'.

Ken Davis *Feelings From Within* (IQ Music)
Feelings from Within opens with sea-wave effects and mewing seagulls. Strands of synthesiser music wash through and gradually the waves dissipate. The tone now becomes more mellow and the music has a lilting effect – urging the listener to become more relaxed. Chimes are introduced and the music acquires an even more assuring and soothing quality. There is a whimsical, light-hearted sequence and the composition then closes on a very gentle level: one simply floats away

on waves of sound.

Side Two opens in a most elegant fashion, with muted piano, and the music flows like a gentle country stream, lapping its way through a meadow. Later it becomes more complex, even oriental in style, but it still retains its relaxing qualities. After a time the music acquires a quicker pace – rather like Mike Oldfield's *Incantations*, and every bit as good. The composition then closes with deep, broad waves of muted synthesiser culminating in a short sequence of expressive piano.

Deuter *Nirvana Road* (Kuckuck)
Georg Deuter – or to give him his complete religious name, Swami Chaitanya Hari Deuter – has for many years composed and recorded beautiful meditative music. His earlier albums include *Aum*, which mixed synthesiser with the sounds of the sea, *Celebration*, featuring bells and bird-songs, and *Ecstasy*, with evocative flute and guitar. *Nirvana Road* is an album so broad in its scope that it is likely to appeal to fans of Gheorghe Zamfir, James Galway and the Chieftains, as well as New Age enthusiasts.

Nirvana Road, for the most part, contains vibrant celebratory music and much of it is in the style of compositions recorded at Rajneeshpuram, where Deuter lived for several years as a follower of the Bhagwan. This album was recorded in California and features two other musicians: Renu on harp and Sebastiano on tabla. Deuter himself plays a wide range of both Indian and western instruments from sitar to acoustic guitar and synthesiser.

Tracks like 'Stairway' and 'Alpine Shadow' – a harp instrumental with a pure, crystalline quality – simply pulse with life. More surprisingly perhaps, many of the tracks also have something of a Celtic feel to them and are reminiscent of the flute and Aeolian pipe tradition which has re-emerged from Ireland with James Galway and the Chieftains. 'Connemara' acknowledges this influence and features a beautiful, trilling pipe-melody. The same quality comes through on 'The High Road' and 'Pacifica'.

Deuter has also been strongly influenced by the East, and several tracks on the second side show this aspect of his work. 'Meadows and Mystics' blends guitar and synthesiser with what sounds very much like sitar or sarod (Deuter's instruments are not identified on the sleeve) and 'Echoes of the East' has a distinctly Indian flavour, with rapid strumming, frenetic tablas and mantric voices which rise up through the music like ancient memories. 'Caravan', too, is an evocative composition, opening with a musical sequence that suggests the plodding lope of camels across the desert. Tablas provide the rhythm and the music gradually increases in tempo as Renu's harp becomes dominant and weaves up and down on Eastern melody scales.

Deuter is equally capable of reflective introspection or expressing life as a celebration. 'Cathedral', a short piece, is dignified and mysterious, while 'Nirvana Road', features vibrant pipes and flute above a dancing synthesiser rhythm. niscent of Mike Oldfield's *Incantations*. Deuter's compositions are indeed bursting with life and light.

Paul Fitzgerald and Mark Flanagan *Quiet Water* (New World)
Very beautiful, graceful music that radiates with a gentle glow, enfolding your whole being in softness and daydreams. Played in a uniquely meditative and reflective style, the softest touch of strings and melodious guitars gently bathe you in sound. Incredibly restful.

Philip Glass *Koyaanisqatsi* (Island)
This album of remarkable impressionistic synthesiser music is the soundtrack of the film of the same name. One of the most beautifully visual films in recent years. *Koyaanisqatsi* was conceived by the Italian-American photographer Godfrey Reggio, and contrasts the rhythms and textures of Nature with the frenzy and artificiality of city life. The images are distinctly separate – we begin with desert vistas, majestic waterfalls and clouds lapping up against mountains and gradually intensify the pace with a visual montage of frenetic freeway traffic, fast-food production chains, and atomic explosions. Which leads us to the title of the film: 'Koyaanisqatsi' is a Hopi Indian expression meaning 'life out of balance'.

Glass' music was written to accompany the visual images in the film and similarly alternates from majestic tonal colours and regal chants through to up-tempo, disorienting music appropriate to the pace of the city. Much of the music is very beautiful and could be used for meditation. The title track and the very impressive composition 'Prophecies' are both in this genre, while tracks like 'The Grid' are intense and dramatic, reinforcing the imagery of life in the fast lane.

Philip Glass already had an international reputation as a new wave composer – established with such works as *Music in 12 Parts, Einstein on the Beach* and *Satyagraha* – and *Koyaanisqatsi* has enhanced his standing even further. Highly recommended.

Chris Glassfield *Island* (New World)
A collection of carefree and flowing melodies, a delightful series of romantic guitar compositions that open our senses to an 'island of relaxation', a land of reflective beauty and peace. Reminiscent of sunwarmed evenings, soft shadows and secret smiles. *Island* is tranquil and refreshingly pure. The music is delicate and superbly played, and sparkles with a clarity that is at the same time intimate and inspiring.

Med Goodall *Emergence* (New World)
A spacious and uplifting recording, alive with a delicate energy and delightfully

sparkling melodies. Clear guitars and flute interlace with keyboard and strings, immersing you in a warm and sensuous bath of music, ideal for relaxing and renewing you at the end of a long day. Inspirational, passionate, lovingly expressive and above all profoundly beautiful, this music is recommended for both its beauty and its calming power.

Srila Gurudeva *Songs of Harmony* and ***Songs of the Soul*** (New World)
The orchestral beauty of this music is only surpassed by the entrancing Oriental songs and superb vocal quality. The music lifts and dances its way into the realm of the soul. Softly stirring, gently joyous, it bestows its gift of spiritual surrender. A beautiful and positive listening experience.

Malcolm Harrison *Freefall* (Phoenix Music)
Freefall is melodic and very much in a contemporary style – it isn't strictly relaxation or meditation music for, rather than becoming muted or overly introspective, it is in fact rich in imagery and colour, and at times quite exuberant.

'Guitar Down' features a beautiful melody line on piano which is later amplified with synthesiser. This is followed by 'Celeste', which has a brisk introduction leading to exquisite sequences of crystalline piano, pulsing synthesiser, wave effects and bells. There are interesting changes of mood as the music alternates between a gentle and vibrant mode.

'Night Flight to Berlin' is optimistic and cheerful and the synthesiser at times sounds like a viola. The blend of piano and keyboards, once again, adds a rich quality to the composition.

On 'Sky Castles' Malcolm opens with acoustic guitar and then leads again into piano and strings. The music has a haunting, evocative quality – like memories floating by in the wind. 'Freefall' begins tentatively but builds to a type of breakthrough point – the music then floats free in a more relaxed style. Adventures of a Snowflake', meanwhile, opens with delicate piano and builds a pattern of crisp and expressive melancholy lines over some mysterious chanting – an attractive and intriguing combination.

Malcolm Harrison will hopefully become more recognised for his music. *Freefall* is an excellent introduction to his distinctive style.

Alan Hinde *The Twilight of Dreams* (New World Productions)
Alan Hinde is one of the most recent arrivals on the Australian New Age music scene. While *The Twilight of Dreams* is understated and somewhat akin to Steven Halpern's minimal style of music, Hinde's background and personal interests have been quite diverse, encompassing classical music and jazz.

The music on this cassette was played on a Yamaha DX7 synthesiser and runs for 30 minutes on each side – which is rather good value these days. Mellow and gentle, it was actually recorded during two meditation sessions, which gives it an added dimension. *The Twilight of Dreams* is very effective as a meditative backdrop and will prove popular with therapists using progressive relaxation as part of their approach.

Recommended.

Les Hurdle and Thor Baldursson *The Secret Melody, The Melody of Life, Creation* and *The Ultimate Melody* (New World)

The Secret Melody Elegant melodies interlace with delightful, tender tones to create a calm environment. This album provides an excellent background for study, contemplation or relaxed activity.

The Melody of Life Designed to uplift and inspire the human spirit, this recording is a real work of art. There is a sensitive, deeply meditative pan pipe that hovers through the music, adding its immanently peaceful, lingering quality. The whole recording is wonderfully refreshing – at times dreamy and sensuous, and at other times sparkling and delightfully inventive.

Creation An intriguing and beautiful musical interpretation of the creation of the World. Streams of lively music and delightful rhythms create an optimistic and relaxing soundscape.

The Ultimate Melody An unusual, exciting and compelling recording. With its even rhythm and sustained melody it has been designed to assist in creating a unique ambience for love-making.

Japetus *The Great, Great Silence, Once Around the Sun* and *Visions of Paradise* (Listen Music)

The Great Great Silence sets a very high standard indeed. Written specifically to accompany meditation, it explores several aspects of self-realisation. Side One, 'Morning', opens with an exquisite sense of expectation – the synthesiser is muted and delicate and the intention is to help the meditator explore different realms of consciousness. Japetus then lifts us through the chakras, taking us further into the inner spaces of the mind. The composition concludes with an intermittent pulse that can be used to focus awareness.

'Evening', on Side Two, opens with soaring, urgent sounds (the city about to subside into darkness?) which soon give way to a feeling of tranquillity. Again there are remarkable ethereal textures and, somewhat like early Klaus Schulze, an exploration of steady, undulating rhythms.

Once Around the Sun presents a more dynamic, primal quality. Japetus wrote the title track to 'capture the grandeur of a planet circling the sun in a seasonal framework, melded with the theme of the life, death and rebirth of its inhabitants'. At first the music is rich and strong – suggestive of bright radiance across an arid landscape. Later it becomes more vibratory and muted as it explores cyclic permutation.

'Rainbow Serpent' is full of the evocative sounds of the outback and would be ideal music for summoning a totem animal! 'Tai Chi Ch'uan' is less successful because while it captures the oriental mystique, its crystalline trilling effects seem out of character with the essentially flowing quality of Tai Chi movements. By contrast, 'Eclipse', which follows, is beautifully expansive and has a rich, soaring quality as does the concluding composition, 'Magnathea' which Japetus says – tongue in cheek – was conceived as 'mood music for extra-terrestrial visitors to pipe through to us as they bring their spaceships in to land on earth.'

The compositions on *Visions of Paradise* are perhaps more varied and more stylistically developed than on the earlier cassettes, and there is something for everyone.

'Gateway' features a dramatic 'orchestral' treatment with flourishes of harp sounds over a pulsing bass rhythm, while 'Adrift' is a free-form composition which washes through your mind casting memories to a far horizon. 'Devotion' is haunting and mysterious – at times the synthesiser sounds like angelic choirs and the music wouldn't be out of place in a Russian Orthodox Church.

The second side opens with 'Cascade', featuring beautiful synthesised piano. The track is reminiscent of Kitaro although Japetus says he had not heard the music of this distinguished Japanese musician until recently and had come to a similar style coincidentally. 'Bliss' is a shimmering haze of sound and becomes increasingly atmospheric, while 'Crystal Dance' has a melodic, optimistic feel to it and closes the album on a revitalising note.

Visions of Paradise is very good indeed.

Karma *Ionospheres* (New World)

Through the use of gentle synthesiser effects and natural sounds, this music explores the inner secrets of Nature, blending the subtle melodies of elemental music with the soothing atmosphere of clouds. The result is a warm and sensual sonic tapestry, a free-floating ambience of harmony that evokes an overwhelming feeling of renewal and well-being. Its unhurried quality lends itself well to unwinding, dreaming or feeling peaceful.

Kitaro *Silver Cloud* (Polygram)

At a time when much of the New Age music is becoming sentimental and repetitive, the Japanese composer Kitaro remains one of the most consistent and distinctive musicians in the genre. Since his early releases, *Oasis* (1979) and *Silk Road* (1980), Kitaro has developed a style of beautiful, lilting synthesiser music which owes more to elegant melodies than to abstract texture and pulsing rhythms. *Silver Cloud* is very much in this style. Several tracks have a regal, almost ceremonial, quality – 'Earth Born' and 'Never Let You Go' for example, are New Age compositions that would seem quite at home in a cathedral setting. At other times Kitaro shows a more intricate approach. The melodies on 'Flying Cloud' dance across the sky and there are attractive crystalline effects on 'Noah's Ark'. Kitaro also explores siren-like sounds on 'Panorama' and blends acoustic guitar with synthesiser on 'Straight A Way to Orion', *Silver Cloud* also includes tracks like 'Return to Russia', which summon a sense of the former imperial majesty, and 'Dreams Like Yesterday', which could easily be a composition for a feature film. So it is perhaps only a matter of time before Kitaro, like Jean Michel Jarre and Vangelis before him, is discovered by the world at large.

Indeed, there are signs already that Kitaro is broadening the scope of his audience. In January 1981 his music was used as a backdrop for a national transmission from snowy Yasaka Village and in March the same year he presented music for a live fashion show which reached 16 million people in Japan.

In 1982 he also performed with the London National Philharmonic Orchestra and has since produced a soundtrack for the movie 'Queen Millennia' with the Los Angeles Symphonic Orchestra. Kitaro is a musician on the verge of international recognition. If you would like to sample some of his finest music, *Silver Cloud* is a good place to begin.

Nicholas Land *The Seasons, Night Echoes* and *Shimmering Moon*
(New World)

The Seasons Tracing its way through the seasons of the year, this special recording from the talented young composer Nicholas Land contains a wonderful variety of memorable and tuneful melodies. Some pieces are subtle and mellow, others are alive with a refreshing and joyous rhythm.

Night Echoes Through light melodies and a sensitive attunement to Nature, this gently flowing synthesiser music explores the beauty of the countryside at night. Delicate and harmonious, with a warm expressive quality, it is very effective for relaxation or for a quiet evening's entertainment.

Shimmering Moon Gently melodic and effortless musical compositions that are both atmospheric and enjoyable.

Larkin *O'cean* (Wind Sung Sounds)

The Californian flautist Larkin calls himself an 'instrument of the wind' and his very beautiful music is a testimony to that.

O'cean has already become legendary for the way in which Larkin's flute blends with the sounds of humpback whales. The music is an elegant blend of wind instrument, synthesiser and watery textures, and Larkin recorded it while watching the flowing movements of a dancer. For this reason 'Emergence' has a special intuitive quality as streams of pure flute music float out over the water like an ancient evocation. Larkin himself calls it, 'an expression of a symbolic language which is telling a story... a new mythology, a new way of looking at the world'. The second side, 'Communitizing', is free-form flute and has a more 'airy' texture, at times providing a sense of soaring inspiration. Larkin describes it as a 'flute dance' although it is lilting rather than frenzied. Those who like Paul Horn's flute album *Inside the Great Pyramid* will appreciate this very much.

Michael Law *The Glass Isle* (New World)
Monumental and entrancing, *The Glass Isle* has its roots in the well-loved, mystical land of Avalon. Michael's profound attunement to 'The Glass Isle' has produced this incredible tape, colourfully interwoven with sinuous sounds and gliding strings. Like a timeless river, this music reveals a world of magic and ancient legend, still relevant to our present dreams and future realities.

Ray Lynch *The Sky of Mind* and *Deep Breakfast* (Ray Lynch Recordings)
One of the most talented New Age musicians in a long time, Ray Lynch has taken quite a while to gain recognition but that should change soon. The refreshing thing about Ray Lynch is that his music is not simply a product of electronic technology but is the end-result of a mature musical background. Trained in classical guitar and music theory, Lynch studied composition at the University of Texas and played lute with the Renaissance Quartet in New York. As one would expect, his music has considerable flair and spontaneity as well as a fine sense of structure and progression. The music also has a joyous, mystical orientation – the American spiritual teacher Da Free John has been a major influence on his work.

Recorded in 1983, Lynch's first album *The Sky of Mind* featured a wide range of instruments, including synthesiser, piano, guitar, Tibetan bells, flute, recorder, cello and violin. Despite this diversity it is less experimental than his more recent work, but nevertheless has considerable appeal.

Sky is essentially a modern interpretation of classical and folk themes. 'Good News', with its acoustic guitar, recorder and flute, is very much in the medieval folk tradition, while 'Quandra', 'Too Wounded' and 'Pavane' develop into rich orchestral compositions. 'The Temple', with its layers of voices, could easily have been inspired by Ligeti.

Lynch's more recent release *Deep Breakfast*, however, is altogether different: a musical breath of fresh air. Several of the tracks are whimsical and light-hearted while others – like 'Kathleen's Song' – feature beautiful viola and lute, and reflect the artist's Renaissance interests.

On the carefree side of the spectrum we find 'Celestial Soda Pop' and 'Rhythm in the Pews' – both of which are delightfully cheerful and bouncy. And another composition, 'Feeling in the Garden', has what one American reviewer called a 'dreamy music-box sound.'

Elsewhere Lynch explores tactile musical effects. 'The Oh of Pleasure', for example, sounds something like cleaning your teeth with a laser beam!

But *Deep Breakfast*, like its predecessor, also has its regal moments. 'Tiny Geometries' begins with watery echoes and flows into a gracious blend of rich tonal colours. Highly recommended.

Robert Martin *Great Peace* (New World)

An inner journey, a very personal and direct experience of Paradise. This is inspired music, a delicate reminder of our links with Nature. Flute, guitar and muse-like angelic choirs translate that experience into an unforgettable affirmation for a Peaceful Planet.

Terry Oldfield *Cascade* and *Reverence* (New World)

Cascade Haunting flute and pan-pipes, distant bird calls, gentle echoes of crystal-clear sounds and celestial effects weave in and out of your senses like sunflecked butterflies; wooing you into their restful, leafy groves. Majestic and moving, *Cascade* is the gift of inspired spirituality, working through the mastery of one of the most skilled and talented composers of our time.

Reverence This album is impeccable, with pure flute interlaced with majestic whale songs, creating a touching dialogue between Man and Nature. Deeply moving, mysterious and endlessly delightful, this album reaffirms our links and empathy with these intelligent sea creatures that share our planet. The whale songs radiate a peaceful, trusting, loving energy, and Terry's superb performance and composition answer in the same tone.

John Richardson *The Response, Cirrus, The Calling, Solstice, Spirit of the Redman* (two cassettes) and ***Devotion*** (New World)

The Response Written with genuine inspiration and reverence for all that is sacred and divine, this haunting music summons up an overwhelming feeling of renewal and wellbeing. Through beauty, through inner peace, emotions are stirred, longings are renewed and love is reawakened. Strings, harpsichord and flute dance through your emotions with a joyful serenity, creating a very special mood.

Cirrus A soothing cyclic pattern, composed to assist with sleep induction and a state of calm relaxation – perfect for massage, healing or relaxed activity.

The Calling Flute and violin combine to create a pure and sacred moment, a direct channel for inspiration – dedicated to Nature and love. *The Calling* was designed to still the mind and achieve harmony with the spirit of the universe – and one certainly leaves this music refreshed and delighted. Richly textured, melodious, intricate and full of images, it radiates grace and serenity, offering its strength and support whenever you feel low. A very enjoyable and enchanting tape, a sublime experience.

Solstice This album was composed specifically to enhance the healing process and to relax the listener during massage or leisure. To this end, the music spirals towards a heavenly space, where celestial voices, comforting and reassuring, ripple gentle in your mind, soothing away all cares and stresses and balancing your deepest energies.

Spirit of the Redman A unique and powerful recording featuring spiritual chants of the American Indian. This music has a deep rhythm and is both joyful and inspirational. A moving and beautiful musical experience that you will not forget. We recommend it highly.

Spirit of the Redman Vol 2 A direct experience of the power of rhythm and chant. The drum beats are unbelievable! There is a strength and dignity to this music that is both enjoyable and energising.

Devotion A unique recording of inspired chanting that radiates a purity of heart and a sense of attunement. Side One is joyous and uplifting, a vibrant song to the beauty of life and love. Side Two is heavenly and expansive, the perfect companion to meditation. Deeply moving and tender, John's voice is used as a beautiful instrument, overflowing with devotion and spiritual inspiration.

Kim Robertson *Wind Shadows, Water Spirit* and ***Moonrise*** (New World)

Wind Shadows The unique sound of the harp, with its warm lingering effect, has been used for thousands of years to soothe and heal, and these calming compositions, radiating clarity, grace and serenity, remain unexcelled. Elegant and uplifting, beautifully clear and delicate, this is a superb recording.

Water Spirit A delightful tape of fresh and fluent harp music, sparkling and poetic. Rippling waves of sound wash over you, providing an ambience of harmony and tranquillity conducive to relaxing and reducing the stresses of daily life.

Moonrise An outstanding recording of peaceful Celtic harp music, specifically intended to be healing, balancing and meditative. Kim's playing is full of feeling and sensitivity, and the impeccable sound quality gives the entire recording a crystal clear presence.

Mike Rowland *Solace, The Fairy Ring* and ***Silver Wings.*** (New World)

Solace *Solace* bathes the listener in a warm caress of sound, and touches one with true peace. It is endlessly pleasing, perfect for healing, relaxation and massage.

The Fairy Ring Inspired by a sensitive attunement to the forces of Nature, these improvisations seem to float in the air while gently revolving around a core of soft melodies and wistful harmonies.

Silver Wings A delightful work of ethereal sensitivity. On opening, one is instantly transported to realms of legendary beauty. A tape to evoke, to move, to haunt. Incredibly beautiful.

David Satchell *Images* and *The Experience* (New World)

Images Suspended in a wash of drifting strings, David's haunting guitar and delightfully clear soft melodies drift through your mind, touching you like a beautiful dream and speaking to you of all loves and emotions, of faraway places and infinite possibilities.

The Experience Light, elegant guitars that lift you out of the ordinary, immersing you in the luxurious environment of 'inner peace'. Surrounded by restful, clear melodies, hovering tones and images wash over you, bathing your imagination in a world of calm waters and radiant skies. Beautifully emotive music that is both pleasurable and richly atmospheric.

Klaus Schulze *Audentity* (Innovative Communications)

Meditation and relaxation music may seem to be a recent development but in fact the roots of this genre go back well over a decade. In the early 1970s Klaus Schulze was a member of Ash Ra Tempel, one of the German groups who, together with Tangerine Dream and Peter Michael Hamel, pioneered the rise of 'inner space' music. Schulze left Ash Ra Tempel and has been releasing albums under his own name since 1972. Some of his most beautiful albums – especially *Mirage* and *Moondawn* – have wonderful meditative tracks and are especially suited to guided imagery visualisation. Since the mid 1970s Schulze has begun to explore more varied electronic effects and his music has become more complex. However, as *Audentity* shows, it is still very interesting.

This album features Klaus Schulze on synthesiser, Rainer Bloss on glockenspiel, Michael Shrieve on percussion and Wolfgang Tiepold on cello. Much of the basic patterning in the music is computer-controlled and the album was digitally recorded in London. There is, nevertheless, a place for appropriate technology and Schulze's music is not as mechanistic as one might expect.

'Amourage' on Side One is a fascinating montage of liquid sounds and has an appealing, serene quality. There are also reflective sequences in the main composition, 'Sebastian im Traum'. Elsewhere on the album Schulze and his fellow musicians explore dramatic percussion effects and musical images of city life. The reason for these contrasts can be found in the fact that the album presents a process of self-transformation. The first tracks reflect the childhood of Sebastian – who is no doubt Schulze himself – and show a variety of influences. 'Opheylissem', for example, is full of the frenetic energy of youth. 'Spielglocken', on the other hand, has a complex urban feeling to it and makes use of interesting digital drum effects.

Later, as Sebastian ventures into more exploratory, creative areas, the music becomes more intuitive and haunting, enhanced especially by wonderful effects from Tiepold on cello.

Audentity, as its composer says on the sleeve notes, is an expression of the search for self-identity. As a musical journey it is well worth listening to.

Stairway *Aquamarine* (New World)

Aquamarine Stilling and captivating, *Aquamarine* emerges from the most endearing of sounds, the voice of the Dolphin. Rippling strings, guitar and breathtaking keyboard announce an enthralling experience, a calm, unhurried voyage to the music of the oceans. Gentle, transparent whispers fascinate your senses and wash away all stress. Softly playful, delicate and relaxing, this music has a warm expressive quality that beckons the listener to a receptive and serene state of awareness.

David Sun *An Island Called Paradise, The Secret Garden, Sunrise, Sunset, Deep Enchantment, Tranquility, Serenity, Peace* and ***Harmony.*** (New World)

An Island called Paradise A tiny tropical South Sea island, with the clear blue sea rolling gently onto the beach, the cool shade of the palm trees – and one hears the soft exotic call of native birds, with the beautiful solo passages of the Bird of Paradise. Sensitively enriching this setting, the tender tones of flute and shimmering, harp-like guitar all subtly blend to create the peaceful dream of 'an island called Paradise'. All around is an aura of contentment and stillness, with the pure meditative flute music hovering in this natural setting, spreading a comforting warmth over the listener.

The Secret Garden Enter an enchanted world of gentle sounds as this soft, tranquil music weaves a path towards your innermost being. The lightest touch of guitar strings seems to hover and balance on the murmur of a garden stream. Birdsongs beckon you closer as the gentle caress of the music awakens inner senses.

Sunrise An elevating and enthralling masterpiece of tranquil music. The gentle blend of serene piano and strings uplift you with crystal-clear sounds into a world of living melodies, where daily cares and stresses are melted away at the touch of its pure and radiant beauty.

Sunset Sensitive and harmonious. Sunset embraces all that is peaceful and sublime. Hovering, tender melodies blend with celestial harp and angelic voices to enfold you in an aura of warmth and rest.

Deep Enchantment A mysterious and subtle musical adventure into the realm of the Unicorn. Silvery sound effects and ethereal tonal textures take the listener through other worlds, where magic is everywhere, weaving in and out of the air itself.

Tranquility A gentle stream of music that floats upon one's own consciousness with barely a ripple. A centred, reflective continuity is maintained throughout as the music hovers with an almost cosmic sense of tranquillity. It has a dreamlike quality, a delicate transparent purity that contains many healing qualities.
Serenity This is certainly some of the best music we've ever heard for meditation, healing or relaxed listening enjoyment. Extremely peaceful and enjoyable throughout, there is a magic and serenity in this music that has not been surpassed. Hauntingly beautiful keyboard seems to drift on the ripples of the lightest wash of 'healing sound', melting the listener into a world of inner rest and contentment. This is spiritual music in the purest sense, heart centering and loving.
Peace Meditative, gentle and totally harmonious throughout. *Peace* is an extraordinarily beautiful and calming recording. Its dreamy relaxed tempo and its delicate tones create an aura of stillness and timelessness, an indescribable sense of balance and well-being. This is deeply restful music, perfect as a gentle background for meditation, conversation, or to create a peaceful home environment.
Harmony This is an expansive tape and yet one that gathers together the feelings of all that is good in Nature. It reaffirms Man's link with the richness of life. It represents the wonders of creation and,through beauty and music, it seeks to enhance our happiness and contact with our inner forces. With its soothing harp and exalting flute, *Harmony* creates a serene and calming ambience.

Phil Thornton *Edge of Dreams* (New World)

Edge of Dreams Misty visions and floating memories are conjured up, only to give way to worlds of indescribable beauty. Bright melodies leisurely develop from gentle strings, soothing harps, a haunting oboe and a distant Chinese gong, majestically producing a most unforgettable dreamscape, where you are the artist and the planner of your dreams.

Tim Wheater *Awakenings, The Enchanter* and ***A Calmer Panorama*** (New World)

Awakenings New Age meditation music has brought to the fore many wonderful flautists, among them Paul Horn, Larkin and Kay Gardner. English musician Tim Wheater must be added to the list. His cassette *Awakenings* is a fine blend of pure melodic flute and gentle, undulating synthesiser – timeless music intended for relaxation and inspiration.

Unlike Paul Horn and Larkin, whose music tends to be abstract and improvised, Tim Wheater's compositions have clear melody lines and seem to draw as much on the Romantic and chamber music traditions as New Age ambience – an intriguing and interesting blend of old and new.

For the most part the music on *Awakenings* is understated and flows at an easy, tranquil pace. The title track is in this style and so too are 'Dolente' with its hint of medieval pageantry, and 'English Serenade' with its sensitive and delicate flute melody. 'Venice' has an orchestral backing and would make excellent theme music for a film, and 'North Star' conjures an introspective mood with its rich blend of flute and synthesiser.

Among the more unusual compositions are 'Perfumed Garden', with bird-chirpings and other Nature sounds integrated with the flute, and 'A Quiet Day' which introduces flute over staccato strings. Tim Wheater gradually builds a fabric of tonal colour, layer by layer, and the effect is most pleasing.

Not all of the tracks are equally successful. 'Running Springs', with its bubbling, rumbling synthesiser rhythms, is some-what eccentric and several of the compositions are rather short: it would have been nice if they could have lasted for longer. But even with these points in mind, there are many fine compositions in the collection and Tim Wheater's music is both expressive and sensitive in its interpretation.

'Sparkling Waters', with its intriguing blend of synthesiser, flute and vibratory effects, is especially appealing, as is 'The Wanderer' – a composition which captures a feeling of freedom and enquiry while still retaining a sense of harmony and peace. It is in fact this capacity to blend and integrate which makes Tim Wheater such an interesting musician. *Awakenings* is a fine introduction to his work.

The Enchanter A dazzling, magical, evocative piece of music, a kaleidoscope of sound which weaves through the emotions in glorious splendour. Inspired by the timeless legends of Merlin – King Maker, Bard, Enchanter – this music remains a monumental celebration to life. Full of the most haunting melodies and exquisite flute sounds imaginable, Tim's unsurpassed flute playing spins a web of multi-textured music that creates a spell of myth, history and beauty.
A Calmer Panorama Exquisitely beautiful flutes that continuously ebb and flow, blending harmoniously with the natural music of falling water and calling birds.

Clifford White *Ascension* and ***Spring Fantasy*** (New World)
Ascension is a hauntingly beautiful album. Clifford White is a master of intriguing melody lines, as on 'Golden Sunrise' and 'Journey's End', but also explores a wide range of musical tones and textures with his electronic equipment. 'The Calling' has an orchestral quality and its melody line suggests a glockenspiel. 'Church of Light' is regal and most attractive, with its harp-like introduction and rich layers of synthesiser, while 'Hallowed Ground' is full of mystery – the music seems to rise up from the earth as if in awesome revelation. 'Ascension' itself is almost a type of 'Moonlight Sonata', and ethereal tones are added to give considerable depth to the composition. Overall, a fine album and one which is thoroughly recommended.
Spring Fantasy An unusual, exciting and totally compelling recording, a musical

exploration of the many moods of Spring; from gentle floating harmonies to joyous celebration, from moments of transcendental beauty to breathtaking and wondrous special effects and natural sounds. An outstanding recording, both for its inventive, alluring nature and for its radiant vitality.

Arden Wilken *Music for Healing, Dream Time, Inner Focus, Music for Children* and ***Inner Harmony.*** (New World)

Music for Healing Arden Wilken is an American-born therapist who now lives on a boat in the Mediterranean and uses music as part of the healing process. A graduate from the University of Washington, Arden became interested in meditation and is especially involved in using her music to tap the inner self. Her recording *Music for Healing*, composed on a Yamaha DX-7 synthesiser, is in the abstract, minimal style – with more emphasis on a flow of soothing textures than on specific melodies. She describes her music as 'droplets of sounds that soothe and renew you in times of stress, relaxing and balancing the body, mind and spirit'. At times her music has a vibratory, chime-like effect, and is both subtle and lilting. It is ideal as a background for practitioners of intuitive massage, spiritual healing or rebirthing and, of course, meditation.

Dream Time Music for Sleep – To sleep healthily, both the mind and the body need to be at rest. Side One has been composed to calm the mind into a state of stillness. Side Two is gentle music to lull you to sleep.

Inner Focus Music for Meditation – Designed to focus the mind – firstly by allowing the brain to 'let go' of all the accumulated stresses of the day, and then by providing an environment for calm 'inner focus'.

Music for Children Side One. Day Play. A gentle, creative flow of music to inspire children through their daily adventures. Side Two. Night Rest. Music for the end of the day, to allow the child to complete the day and drift off to sleep.

Inner Harmony Light and delicate tones that generate a gentle energy, and then sensitively guide you towards a state of stillness and inner calm. This recording reflects Arden's unique ability to be able to 'tune into' an individual, and through sound and music, to relax and balance them.

Contacts for further information:

New World Cassettes
PO Box 15
Twickenham TW1 4SP
Middlesex
England

New World Productions
PO Box 244
Red Hill
Brisbane 4059
Queensland
Australia

Lotus Music Pty Ltd
PO Box 2
Woollahra
NSW 2025
Australia

Music from the Hearts
of Space
PO Box 31321
San Francisco
California.
U.S.A.

APPENDIX B: MUSIC AND THE ELEMENTS – A CHECKLIST

Music for Entering an Altered Stated (General):

Peter Baumann, 'Meadow of Infinity' (Part One), 'The Glass Bridge' and 'Meadow of Infinity' (Part Two), from *Romance 76* (Virgin)
Cluster & Eno, 'Ho Renomo' from *Cluster & Eno* (Sky)
Lol Creme and Kevin Godley, 'Fireworks', 'Burial Scene' (instrumental sequences only), 'Sleeping Earth' and 'The Flood' from *Consequences* (Mercury)
Eno, Moebius and Roedelius, 'Foreign Affairs' from *After the Heat* (Sky)
Philip Glass, *Koyaanisqatsi* (entire album) (Island)
Philip Glass, 'Part I' from *Music in 12 Parts* (Virgin)
Claire Hammill, *Voices* (entire album) (Coda)
Jon Hassell and Brian Eno, 'Charm' from *Possible Musics Vol. I* (EG/Polygram)
Gyorgy Ligeti, 'Requiem' and 'Lux Aeterna' from *2001* soundtrack (MGM)
Herbie Mann, 'Shomyo (Monks' Chant)', from *Gagaku & Beyond* (Finnadar)
Japetus, *The Great, Great Silence* (entire cassette) (Listen Music)
Klaus Schulze, 'Voices of Syn' from *Blackdance* (Virgin)
Klaus Schulze, 'Trancefer' (Side One) from *Trancefer* (Innovative Communication)

Music for the Element Earth:

Chaitanya Hari Deuter, *Ecstasy* (entire album) (Kuckuck)
Brian Eno, *Ambient Four: On Land* (entire album) (EG/Polygram)
Philip Glass, 'Koyaanisqatsi' from *Koyaanisqatsi* (Island)
Michael Hoenig, 'Hanging Garden Transfer' from *Departure from the Northern Wasteland* (Warner Bros.)
Paul Horn, 'Psalm 4 – Enlightenment' from *Inside the Great Pyramid* (Mushroom)
Kitaro, 'Cosmic Energy' from *Oasis* (Kuckuck)
Jade Warrior, 'Waves Part II' (first third) from *Waves* (Island)
Herbie Mann, 'Shomyo' from *Gagaku & Beyond* (Finnadar)
Rajneesh Foundation musicians, 'Nadabrahma' (first two-thirds) from *Nataraj/ Nadabrahma* (Rajneesh Foundation International)
Klaus Schulze, 'Conphara' and 'Chromengel' from *Cyborg* (Ohr), 'Ways of Changes' from *Blackdance* (Virgin), 'Spielglocken' from *Audentity* (Innovative Communication), 'A Few Minutes After Transfer' from *Trancefer* (Innovative Communication)
Tangerine Dream, 'The Big Sleep in Search of Hades' from *Stratosfear* (Virgin), 'Mysterious Semblance at the Strand of Nightmares' from *Phaedra* (Virgin), 'Ricochet, Part I' from *Ricochet* (Virgin), *'Rubycon,* Part I' from Rubycon (Virgin), 'Alpha Centauri' from *Alpha Centauri* (Ohr), 'Nebulous Dawn' from *Zeit* (Ohr/ Virgin), 'Through Metamorphic Rocks' from *Force Majeure* (Virgin), 'Tangram Set

2' from *Tangram* (Virgin)
Yatha Sidhra, 'Part I' from *Meditation Mass* (Brian/Metronome)

Music for the Element Water:

Ash Ra Tempel, 'Jenseits' from *Join Inn* (Ohr)
Brian Eno, *Ambient One: Music for Airports* (first half, first side) (EG/Polygram), *Discreet Music* (first side) (Antilles), 'Inland Sea' and 'Sparrowfall I' from 'Music for Films (EG/Polygram)
Brian Eno and Harold Budd, 'Above Chiang Mai' and 'An Arc of Doves' from *Ambient Two: The Plateaux of Mirror* (EG/Polygram)
Fripp and Eno, 'Wind on Water' from *Evening Star* (Island)
Steve Hillage, 'Garden of Paradise' from *Rainbow Dome Musick* (Virgin)
Jade Warrior, 'Waterfall' and 'Memories of a Distant Sea' from *Floating World* (Island)
Kitaro, 'Oasis' from *Oasis* (Kuckuck)
Larkin, 'Emergence' from *O'cean* (Wind Sung Sounds)
Edgar Froese, 'Aqua' and 'Upland' from *Aqua* (Virgin), 'Epsilon in Malaysian Pale' from *Epsilon in Malaysian Pale* (Virgin)
Herbie Mann, 'Mauve over Blues' from *Gagaku & Beyond* (Finnadar)
Pink Floyd, 'Echoes' (first quarter) from *Meddle* (Harvest), 'Part Seven' from *Wish You Were Here* (Harvest)
Klaus Schulze, 'Bayreuth Return' from Timewind (Virgin), 'Crystal Lake' from *Mirage* (Island), 'Mindphaser' (first half) from *Moondawn* (Brian/Metronome), 'Nowhere – Now Here' from *Body Love* (Island)

Music for the Element Fire:

Ash Ra, 'Sun Rain' from *New Age of Earth* (Virgin)
Manuel Gottsching, 'Echo Waves' from *Invention for Electric Guitar* (Ohr)
Philip Glass, 'The Grid' from *Koyaanisqatsi* (Island)
Kitaro, 'Morning Prayer' from *Oasis* (Kuckuck)
Laraaji, 'Dance 1' and 'Dance 2' from *Ambient Three: Day of Radiance* (EG/Polygram)
Mike Oldfield, 'Part I' from Ommadawn (Virgin), 'Incantations Part 3' from *Incantations* (Virgin)
Klaus Schulze, 'Ways of Changes' from *Blackdance* (Virgin), 'Floating' from *Moondawn* (Brian/Metronome)
Tangerine Dream, 'Force Majeure' (last third) from *Force Majeure* (Virgin), 'Set 1' (first third) from *Tangram* (Virgin), 'Logos' (second half) and 'Logos 2' (middle section) from *Logos* (Virgin)

Music for the Element Air:

Brian Eno, 'Under Stars' and 'Weightless' from *Apollo* (EG/Polygram)
Brian Eno and Harold Budd, 'The Chill Air' and 'Wind in Lonely Fences' from *Ambient Two: The Plateaux of Mirror* (EG/Polygram)
Fripp and Eno, 'Wind on Water' and 'Wind on Wind' from *Evening Star* (Island)
Michael Hoenig, 'Voices of Where' from *Departure from the Northern Wasteland* (Warner Bros.)
Paul Horn, 'Inside' and 'Mumtaz Mahal' from *Inside* (Epic), 'Psalm 2' and 'Psalm 3' (Initiation), 'Psalm 1' and 'Psalm 3' (Meditation), 'Psalm 2' (Enlightenment) and 'Psalm 4' (Fulfilment), from *Inside the Great Pyramid* (Mushroom)
Jade Warrior, 'Clouds' from *Floating World* (Island), 'The Wind Song' from *Kites* (Island)
Japetus, *The Great, Great Silence* (opening sequence) (Listen Music)
Herbert Joos, 'Why?' from *Daybreak* (Japo)
Larkin, 'Communitizing' from *O'cean* (Wind Sung Sounds)
Rajneesh Foundation musicians, 'Nadabrahma' (last third) from *Nataraj/ Nadabrahma* (Rajneesh Foundation International)
Majo Rolyat, 'Sky Bells' from *Music Mantras* (Hermann Bauer Verlag)
Klaus Schulze, 'Wahnfried 1883' from *Timewind* (Virgin)
Jukka Tolonen, 'Mountains' from *Tolonen* (Sonet)

Music for the Element Spirit:

Aeoliah, *The Light of Tao* (second side) (Sona Gaia Productions)
Aeoliah and Larkin, *Inner Sanctum* (entire cassette) (Celestial Octaves)
Ash Ra, 'Ocean of Tenderness' from *New Age of Earth* (Virgin)
Jon Anderson, 'Song of Search' from *Olias of Sunhillow* (Atlantic)
Geoffrey Chandler, *Starscapes* (entire album) (Unity)
Cluster & Eno, 'Wehrmut' from *Cluster & Eno* (Sky)
Brian Eno, *Ambient One: Music for Airports* (last third of first side, second side), 'An Ending (Ascent)' and 'Stars' from *Apollo* (EG/Polygram)
Brian Eno and Harold Budd, 'Falling Light' from *Ambient Two: The Plateaux of Mirror* (EG/Polygram)
Fripp and Eno, 'An Index of Metals' (first quarter) from *Evening Star* (Island)
Edgar Froese, 'Epsilon in Malaysian Pale' (first half) from *Epsilon in Malaysian Pale* (Virgin)
Philip Glass, 'Prophecies' from *Koyaanisqatsi* (Island)
Manuel Gottsching, 'Qasarsphere' from *Inventions for Electric Guitar* (Ohr)
Nancy Hennings and Henry Wolff, 'Astral Plane' from *Tibetan Bells II* (Celestial Harmonies)
Paul Horn, 'Akasha' from *Inside* (Epic)

Jade Warrior, 'Waves, Part II' (last third) from *Waves* (Island)
Larraaji, 'Meditation 1' from *Ambient Three: Day of Radiance* (EG/Polygram)
Gyorgy Ligeti, 'Requiem' and 'Lux Aeterna' from *2001* soundtrack (MGM)
Majo Roylat, 'Confidence' from *Music Mantras* (Herman Bauer Verlag)
Klaus Schulze, 'Velvet Voyage' from *Mirage* (Island)
Tangerine Dream, 'Rubycon II' (first and last section) from *Rubycon* (Virgin), 'Sequent C' from *Phaedra* (Virgin), 'Sunrise in the 3rd System' from *Alpha Centauri* (Ohr), 'Atem' (second half) and 'Circulation of Events' from *Atem* (Ohr), 'Birth of Liquid Pleiades', 'Origin of Supernatural Probabilities' and 'Zeit' from *Zeit* (Ohr/Virgin)

Music Encompassing all Elements:
Steve Hillage, 'For Ever Rainbow' from *Rainbow Dome Musick* (Virgin)
Klaus Schulze, 'Sebastian im Traum' from *Audentity* (Innovative Communication)

Music for Relaxation:
Robert Bearns and Ron Dexter, *Golden Voyage* (4 vols.) (Awakening Productions)
Jon Bernoff and Marcus Allen, *Breathe* (Whatever), *Petals* (Whatever)
Harold Budd, *The Pavillion of Dreams* (EG/Polygram)
Harold Budd and Brian Eno, *The Pearl* (EG/Polygram)
Steven Halpern, *Dawn* (Halpern Sounds), *Eastern Peace* (Halpern Sounds), *Eventide* (Halpern Sounds), *Prelude* (Halpern Sounds), *Spectrum Suite* (Halpern Sounds), *Starborn Suite* (Halpern Sounds), *Zodiac Suite* (Halpern Sounds)
Alan Hinde, *The Twilight of Dreams* (New World Productions)
Kitaro, *Silk Road* (Kuckuck), *Ki* (Kuckuck), *Oasis* (Kuckuck), *Silver Cloud* (Polygram)
David Sun, *Deep Enchantment* (New World)
Clifford White, *Ascension* (New World)
(see other listings in Appendix A)

BIBLIOGRAPHY

Alvin, J., *Music Therapy*, Hutchinson, London, 1975

Assagioli, R., *Psychosynthesis*, Turnstone, London, 1975

Bailey, A., *Esoteric Healing*, Lucis Press, London, 1926

Beasley, V., *Subtle Body Healing*, University of the Trees Press, Los Angeles, 1980

Cade, M., *The Awakened Mind*, Wildwood House, London, 1979

Clynes, M., 'Music Beyond the Score', *Somatics*, Vol.V, No. 1., Autumn-Winter, 1984-85

Clynes, M., (ed.) *Music, Mind and Brain*, Plenum, New York, 1982

Diamond, J., *Life Energy*, Dodd Mead, New York, 1985; Harper & Row, Sydney, 1986

Diamond, J., *Your Body Doesn't Lie*, Harper & Row, Sydney, 1979

Drury, N., (ed.) *Inner Health*, Prism Press, Bridport, Dorset, 1985

Drury, N., *Music for Inner Space*, Prism Press, Bridport, Dorset, 1985

Dychtwald, K., *Bodymind*, Wildwood House, London, 1978

Ferguson, M., *The Aquarian Conspiracy*, Tarcher, Los Angeles, 1980

Grof, S., *Beyond the Brain*, State University Press of New York, Albany, 1985

Halpern, S., *Sound Health*, Harper & Row, San Francisco, 1985

Halpern, S., *Tuning the Human Instrument*, Spectrum Research Institute, Belmont, California, 1978

Hamel, P.M., *Through Music to the Self*, Compton Press, Salisbury, 1978

Jurisevic, S., 'Releasing Emotional Blocks – the Sentic Cycles of Manfred Clynes', *Wellbeing*, Sydney, September-October 1984

Kelly, T., *Teach Yourself Singing*, IWP Publishing, Menlo Park, California, 1980

McAdams, S., 'Spectral Fusion and the Creation of Auditory Images' in M. Clynes (ed.) *Music Mind and Brain*, Plenum, New York, 1982

Mitchell, S., 'Music and Psychological Medicine', *Proceedings of the Royal Medical Association*, LXXVII, London 1951

Nieman, A., *British Journal of Music Therapy*, Vol. IV., No. 3, 1973

Pelletier, K., *Holistic Medicine*, Delta Books, New York, 1979

Pelletier, K., *Mind as Healer, Mind as Slayer*, Delta Books, New York, 1977

Pietroni, P., *Holistic Living*, Dent, London, 1986

Priestley, M., *Music Therapy in Action*, Constable, London, 1975

Rudhyar, D., *The Magic of Tone and the Art of Music*, Shambhala, Boulder, Colorado, 1982

Samuels M. & N., *Seeing with Mind's Eye*, Random House, New York, 1975

Schneider, M., 'Primitive Music' in E. Wellesz (ed.) *Ancient and Oriental Music*, Oxford University Press, Oxford, 1957

Scott. C., *Music: its Secret Influence through the Ages*, Theosophical Publishing House, London, 1937

Seashore, C., *Psychology of Music*, Dover, New York, 1967
Shorr, J.E., (ed.) *Imagery*, Plenum, New York, 1980
Sigerist, H.E., *Civilization and Disease*, University of Chicago Press, Chicago, 1962
Simonton, C. & S., *Getting Well Again*, Bantam, New York, 1980
Tansley, D., *Radionics and the Subtle Anatomy of Man*, Health Science Press, London, 1975
Turner, A., and Hill, S., *Music from the Hearts of Space*, PO Box 31321, San Francisco, 1981
Waters, F., *The Book of the Hopi*, Penguin, Baltimore, 1972
Wechsler, R., 'A New Prescription: Mind over Malady', *Discover*, New York, February 1987
Wilson, A., *What Colour Are You?*, Turnstone, London, 1975